Battling Democracy's Decline

Battling Democracy's Decline:

Lessons From The Trenches

by Michael Mills

ISBN 1-4392-1086-1
Library of Congress Control Number: 2008927932

BookSurge Publishing
1-866-308-6235
www.booksurge.com

Dedication

Dedicated to my grandfather, George Holahan. And to all active citizens toiling to bring about a "government of the people, by the people, and for the people."

Introduction

America is at a crossroads. We face unprecedented threats to our security at home and abroad. The American economy is struggling, and as a result, elected officials at all levels of government are facing tough decisions. But the state of the world in the new millennium provides a tremendous opportunity for citizen engagement and new leadership. However, taking advantage of this opportunity requires that citizens see a connection between government and their daily lives and between voting, participating in the civic process, and creating change.

The crossroads we stand at today is reminiscent of my first adult experience with government and the civic process. The excitement and optimism of the 1992 presidential election is still fresh in my mind more than 15 years later. It was my first opportunity to vote, and I intended to make the most of the experience. But this was more than just an election and a chance to flex my civic muscles for the first time. I was a freshman at Hobart and William Smith Colleges in upstate New York, and the world around me seemed to be moving at a frenetic pace. I was away from home for only the second time in my life, meeting new people, making new friends and delving into the works of Socrates, Plato and other teachers of political philosophy.

The introduction of new environments, relationships and ideas into my life created a tremendous sense of opportunity, unleashing a bright-eyed idealism and hope for leaving my mark on the world. And I wasn't alone. Dorm rooms and common areas all over campus teemed with excitement as the presidential debates unfolded, and a man from Hope, Arkansas, gave a generation hope that civic action could bring about change in the political process.

Bill Clinton was the first candidate in years to speak directly to young people and say, "Your issues are important. Your voice matters. And I want to make sure your action, in the form of votes, brings about a better world for all of us." His appearances on "Arsenio Hall" and "MTV Choose or Lose" forums made government and the civic process real for young Americans. He was the only candidate discussing the environment, crime, student loans, community service and other issues directly relevant to young people. And as a result, America's youth were mobilizing to break from the stereotype of a privileged, lazy and "slacker" generation. We wanted to be heard, and Bill Clinton was listening.

Media pundits, professors and others made parallels between Clinton and his idol, President John F. Kennedy. The latter was a leader who stirred a nation to dream about landing a man on the moon, while getting them to willingly pay any price to ensure freedom around the world. The former was a man inspiring optimism in a new generation of young people. Because of him, young Americans began to believe that they not only deserved, but would actually get a seat at the political table and that all things were possible with determination, hard work and a commitment to service. A palpable current of electricity surged through my campus and others around the nation. Optimism was blossoming. And young people believed a new day was dawning in American government.

Candidate Clinton was our Jack Kennedy. He brought the promise of building a new Camelot: a new America, where service to our communities and public policy went hand in hand, where we openly debated and tackled the tough issues facing our nation. It appeared as if Bill Clinton cared about each of us — and our nation — and would do anything to bring a common-sense, public-policy-based approach to government.

He talked, and a generation was inspired. I voted. And so did 37 percent of eligible 18- to 24-year-olds, the largest youth turnout since 1972 when 18-year-olds earned the right to vote. This surge of youth activism was a key factor in the outcome of the 1992 election. And it ensured an opportunity for the man from Hope to build democracy in our nation and around the world based upon a '60s-style activism of service inspired by ideas. Many of America's youth believed civic service would provide them the opportunity to build stronger communities, which would have a profound effect on the world. And thus, Bill Clinton went to Washington with a generation's hopes and dreams in his hands.

The Clinton era marked the most sustained economic surge in American history and the creation of an army of AmeriCorps volunteers. Nearly 23 million jobs were created during the Clinton years, the most of any single administration. Home ownership levels rose to all-time highs, and the unemployment rate dropped to four percent — the lowest in three decades. And fewer Americans were on welfare than at anytime in the previous 37 years.

Perhaps the most successful program of the Clinton years was the creation of AmeriCorps. This community service program allowed college students to earn money for their education by working in classrooms, helping to ensure public safety or improving the environment through partnerships with nonprofit organizations across the nation. The program enrolled more than 200,000 young people in its first five years, surpassing the combined 40-year roster of Peace Corps workers.

While this is an impressive record, it is diminished, or at least marginalized because of the Clinton era's most prominent legacy — continuous scandal, partisan bickering and ultimately, the threat of impeachment. A generation's hopes and dreams turned to nightmares as the Clinton scandals ushered in a new era of partisanship and a government too busy fighting to achieve anything tangible. Republicans seethed with contempt and anger for a man they believed was soiling the presidency for personal gain and satisfaction. Democrats turned away in droves as each scandal felt more like a paper cut to the soul, eventually bleeding them dry.

My generation turned away as well. They stopped engaging in government activity and turned their attention to more promising personal undertakings, like the Internet and the New Economy. The youngest voters grabbed their boards and rode the waves of a "dot.com explosion," creating entire industries and wealth along the way. Countless others turned to community service as their contribution to the civic good. Either way, millions of young Americans gave up on government.

A 2000 Harvard study analyzing the political attitudes of college students across America brings this point home. Nearly 60 percent of poll participants said the major problems facing America would be solved through volunteerism, not engagement in the political process. More than half of a generation believed government had little meaning to their daily lives. Optimism and action had turned to cynicism and neglect.

This civic neglect is evidenced in the growing lack of interest in, or knowledge of politics and government. A 2000 Community Foundation study found that the percentages of citizens engaged in civic activity or staying informed of current events are dwindling.

In Atlanta, where I've been working in the civic trenches for the past 10 years, nearly two-thirds of those surveyed failed to name one of their two United States senators. This is not intended to disparage the uninformed. Rather, these statistics highlight the severity of the crisis we face in America.

Not one to succumb often to peer pressure, I bucked my generation's increasing departure from the civic process by studying the topic in graduate school and working in state government with the hopes of reengaging people in the political process. That work led me to the political campaign trail, to educating the general public about critical issues, and ultimately, it led me to found the Coalition for a Voting America — a non-partisan organization educating citizens about issues and the civic process.

The power of civic education moved me throughout these experiences. Each phase of my public service helped cement a belief that Americans, for the most part, do want to engage in the civic process. Unfortunately, more often than not, they just don't know how government works or have a clear, unbiased understanding of the issues or candidate's positions. But one thing, above all, was resoundingly clear: Americans are tired of rhetoric and partisanship and want candidates and elected officials to focus on issues and voters.

One experience in particular encapsulates what I saw in the trenches. Civics 101 classes were one of the first programs offered by the Coalition for a Voting America. The program's goal was to help people understand the civic process so they could more efficiently and effectively interact with government, bringing about positive change and common-sense public policy. Each course was broken into three segments: a government primer, issue analysis and a roundtable about community issues and potential solutions. The roundtables always included a panel of elected officials and community activists talking about issues, how government works, why being engaged matters and concrete recommendations for taking action.

One of the participants at our very first Civics 101 class fit the profile of a jaded citizen. She seemed to believe that government is run by corrupt or even inept elected officials who have little relevance to her daily life. This woman was ill-informed about the civic process and hadn't taken the time to get to know her elected officials. As such, she was skeptical when one of our panelists, a senator from the Georgia General Assembly, informed the group that he wanted and needed their input to accurately cast votes across a range of issues. He explained to the group that unlike his counterparts in Washington, members of the General Assembly rely on a small staff to help them navigate the legislative process. This small staff usually includes one administrative assistant who is shared by multiple representatives and a legislative aide — usually a college intern. As a result, he informed the group, it was lobbyists and individual citizens who must provide local legislators with much of the data needed to make informed decisions.

The woman asked the panelists numerous tough questions about the jobs of elected officials and the "real" opportunities for citizen input. It was clear she believed government was beholden to special interests and the power of "a few." But then something amazing happened. I watched as this woman cornered the state senator after the program to continue her stern line of questioning. It was clear from her words, mannerisms and facial expressions that actually meeting an elected official broke down her previously held notions. She began to realize elected officials were indeed accessible and weren't entirely beholden to lobbyists and special interest groups. But more importantly, our program taught her that elected officials do want and need constituent input. This was especially true for officials at the local level who don't have the extensive staff structure of their D.C. counterparts.

The most rewarding and enlightening aspect of that first class came when my phone rang a few weeks later. The woman who gave our panelists such a difficult time called to relay how eye-opening the Civics 101 experience was for her. The program helped her realize that citizen voices do matter in the civic process, which requires informed action by civic leaders. As a result, she began volunteering in the mayor's office of a small suburban city outside Atlanta. The lesson was clear: People will take civic action when they understand how government works and feel invited and empowered to participate in the process.

This book is more than just an analysis of American civic participation. It paints a picture of a citizenry that has removed itself from the process over time because, for many, government is irrelevant and too toxic to be a part of their daily lives. There are countless books that stop there, with the negative story of American civic participation. But this one offers the promise of what can be accomplished by an informed and engaged citizenry. And I hope, this book will provide inspiration for people to take part.

My experience in the trenches of civic activism shows that Americans do care about government and the impact it has on our world. They merely want to be engaged, inspired and invited into the process. Americans want government, at all levels, to be more about results and the bottom line than a battle between political parties trying to score the most partisan points with tired political rhetoric.

I took a different path than many of my contemporaries who left the civic process when their dreams of a new Camelot were shattered. Choosing that path reinforced my belief in the possibilities of a nation of active citizens. Throughout the process, I studied the history of American participation and the previous individual and organizational efforts to increase awareness and involvement. I learned first hand what worked, what didn't and why. I also identified three significant barriers to participation and the steps to reduce the impact of each. All of these experiences and insights are included in the following pages.

As with most problems in our world, there is no magic cure to make more Americans care about government and the issues facing our society. The key is to help them realize that legislation happens — it's just a question of whether it happens with them or to them. Time, hard work, planning and vigilance are the best means at our disposal to make Americans see the critical link between government and their daily lives.

My optimism and idealism, while challenged throughout this journey, are still intact. I truly believe that we can move our nation to action. And through our combined efforts, informed participation will bring about President Abraham Lincoln's vision: "A government of the people, by the people, and for the people."

Recent world events are forcing Americans to reconsider their views of government and their interaction with it. Our economy was humming along for nearly a decade, which allowed government to fix potholes, crumbling infrastructure and other problems with tangible results, and at the same time it was cutting taxes and improving the quality of life for more citizens. But the recession at the start of this decade and the subsequent economic roller coaster is forcing government to cut services. Budgets can't support the benefits enjoyed by citizens a few short years ago. And as a result, elected officials are being forced to make tough decisions such as raising taxes, while reducing government's reach. But the current state of our economy presents a tremendous opportunity for citizens to make their voices heard.

The events of September 11, 2001, also changed the way Americans view government. In the roaring 1990's, we had few worries, let alone the notion that terrorism — experienced around the world for decades — would land on our soil. But that fateful morning woke a sleeping giant. And we responded ferociously to ensure our safety at home and abroad. The resulting War on Terrorism and Operation Iraqi Freedom initially created greater awareness of, and reliance on, government services. People once again celebrated police officers, firefighters and military personnel. We rallied behind them; suddenly cognizant of the sacrifices they make each day to keep us safe. Americans also willingly relinquished some personal freedoms, accepting increased scrutiny at airports and train stations and the occasional closure of national monuments because of terrorist threats.

This post-September 11th world presents numerous opportunities for citizens to be aware of and involved in the civic process. The threat of terror, continued war and increasing tensions in the Middle East, and economic uncertainty are waking Americans to the realization that government done right, and minimally, is a good thing. It protects us from terrorists, keeps our streets clean, delivers our mail, maintains our environment and does countless other things to make our lives better. But with these benefits comes a responsibility for being informed and involved.

We are at a crossroads in America. We face serious challenges domestically and around the globe. We remain at war; the Middle East is ripping apart and countless enemies are rattling their sabers, threatening to attack us around the globe. Citizens can continue to turn away from the civic process, leading to a nation led by a few. Or they can become engaged and make their voices heard.

My hands-on experience with everyday citizens hungering for a voice in their government made it clear that they do want to be involved in the process. They just need help getting started. They need to know that someone in government will listen, that they matter and that their vote counts. They need leaders, elected and otherwise, to help them learn about the process and the issues facing communities. They want a debate about issues, not lip service to progress.

I am hopeful that together, with information, inspiration and perspiration, we can bring about a new day in America. One where people of all ages, races, economic backgrounds and beliefs come together to debate and develop common-sense solutions to the central issues we face today and in the future. I hope this book inspires you to join me in the trenches.

Section I

Chapters 1 – 4

The Greatest Generation:
Civic Role Models

Chapter 1

Introduction to the Greatest Generation

February 21, 2001
Dear George:

It is with great pleasure and a deep sense of pride that I write in honor of this momentous occasion — your 80th birthday. This letter not only commemorates this special day — February 29, 1921 — but also celebrates your life and the example you have set for us all.

Yours is a generation that led our nation through tumultuous times marked by economic depression, international conflict and global uncertainty. It is due to the efforts and sacrifices of the men and women of your generation that has given our country the prosperity and the freedoms we enjoy. In the face of uncertainty and turmoil, the courage and faith of men like you helped to strengthen and solidify America as *the* world power and beacon of democracy that it represents to our global village.

America leads the world in economic, military and cultural prowess. We have a constitutional government that is unique and unparalleled, a political experiment that steadfastly survives despite the trials and tribulations we go through as a nation. But we also have a compassion for those individuals and countries less fortunate than us. Your generation deserves the accolades because it is you who taught us to be forward-thinking for all the world's citizens and the earth itself.

This example, as so well demonstrated by you, inspires the men and women of today to dedicate their lives to service around the world, making this a safer, more prosperous and free place to live. Courage and leadership is evident throughout your life. The courage and commitment you have to the ideals of this land are exemplified in the Bronze Star and Purple Heart medals you earned in the Marine Corps. It is this sincere sense of duty that truly distinguishes you as a man and as an American, George Holahan.

I believe the words of General C.B. Bate, Commandant of the Marine Corps, in his March 2, 1948, letter says it best: "I take pleasure in forwarding to you the enclosed permanent citation for the Bronze Star Medal previously presented by the President of the United States for heroic achievement during operations against enemy Japanese forces on Tarawa, Gilbert Islands, 26 November 1943, with the United States Marine Corps. Be assured of my deep appreciation of your devotion to duty and gallant action which were in keeping with the highest traditions of the United States Marine Corps."

It is my privilege, as your New York State Assemblyman, to extend sincere appreciation and gratitude for 80 years of stoic leadership and dedication to this city, state and our nation. We are all much better off because of your contributions. May your 80th birthday be the best one yet, and may you be surrounded by love, happiness, family and friends.

Best Regards,
Joseph E. Robach, Member of Assembly (*The State of New York*)

We all know a member of the Greatest Generation. They are a mother, father, friend, colleague, brother or grandparent. The best example of the Greatest Generation in my life was George Holahan — my grandfather and my true inspiration for civic engagement. George's state assemblyman sent the letter on the previous page to commemorate his 80th birthday. But it could have been written about thousands of other Americans who grew up during that time.

Like many members of Generation X, the history of my family is becoming difficult to discern as grandparents and other relatives pass away, leaving second-hand memories rather than first hand accounts. However, I have been able to piece together enough of my family's past to know that our story is typical of the Greatest Generation.

My grandfather, George Joseph Holahan was born in Rochester, New York, on February 28, 1921, to William and Mary Holahan. Young George was the last of nine children — a 10th died from whooping cough at a young age. As you can imagine, the last child of a brood that large didn't enjoy a close bond to his parents. They were assuredly tired from the peaks and valleys of raising the eight preceding children.

Closer to the roots of the family tree, George's father William was a second generation American whose family immigrated from Germany and Ireland. William's birth father died, his mother remarried, and they both became Holahans. William married Mary Rettinger and worked in a local bottling plant to provide for his growing family. Like many at the time, they faced particularly hard times during the Great Depression and throughout the following years.

William and Mary's growing family included sons Happy, Hookie, Ray and George. And they had five daughters: Marge, Madge, Kay, Marian and Bernadine. Earning an advanced degree at that time was pretty tough for a boy who was the last of nine in a Depression-era family. Even though college wasn't on the horizon, George worked hard enough to get into the rigorous Aquinas Institute of Rochester, a

Catholic high school. From all indications, he did well, graduating in 1938. He went to work full-time for the Coca-Cola Bottling Company as a truck driver after graduation — a job he began at age 16.

Like most young men of his generation, George watched as World War II raged across the fronts in Europe and the Pacific. Also like many in that generation, George would soon heed the call to action, enlisting in the United States Marine Corps on April 6, 1942. He signed up just as the battle of Midway reached epic proportions. America had committed troops to World War II about six months prior to George's enlisting, which meant he was rushed into training in Austin, Texas. He was trained as a radio specialist in Austin, and was assigned to a bomber group in the Pacific Fleet upon completion of his training.

The Bloody Battle of Tarawa

Humility was a consistent trait among members of the Greatest Generation, preventing them from disclosing much about their combat experience later in life. As we'll see in subsequent chapters, the G.I. Generation saw nothing extraordinary in their accomplishments. And as a result, they tended not to share the details of their war experiences.

My grandfather was no different. He regaled us with stories of big bands and clubs, barroom brawls and socializing stateside. But George rarely shared even the slightest details about his experience overseas. Perhaps it was because of the gruesome nature of war, or because of the constant exposure to danger that forced soldiers to keep these stories bottled up.

It wasn't until I was studying at Hobart that my grandfather finally provided a few details surrounding the events that led to his receiving a Bronze Star for valor. After some research, I realized that he played an early role in the Battle for Tarawa. The conflict was for control of a Japanese-constructed airfield on Betio Island, Tarawa Atoll in the Gilbert Islands. The 4,000-foot runway was a necessary staging area for U.S. troops attempting to secure the Pacific, on their way to Japan. A high price would be paid by U.S. forces in their quest to control the island.

The Second Marine Division trained for months on the beaches of Australia before invading Tarawa. More than 5,000 battle-hardened enemy troops were dug into Tarawa's 300-acres of sand, which was reinforced with palm logs and concrete. The battle got off to a rough start, as Marines waded ashore in a freakishly low tide. This miscalculation of the elements stranded countless landing craft and forced the first wave of Marines to come ashore dangerously exposed and ill-equipped. Yet the soldiers pushed on and were able to land a wave of Marines in amphibious tractors. This tiny toehold of beachfront was directly behind a log seawall that in a few places was no more than 20-feet from the water's edge.

The low tides stranded hundreds of the initial landing crafts on reefs. And the receding waters, which left countless soldiers exposed, were directly responsible for nearly half of the Marine casualties that took place during *the entire* battle. The first waves of attack were hampered by stiff resistance and tactical mistakes that went beyond mere tide miscalculations. The mistakes accounting for hundreds of deaths on Tarawa were so significant that they provided rich lessons to planners of Marine-landing parties in future World War II battles and beyond.

Battleships and cruisers continued to pound Tarawa in an effort to weaken the resistance for the Marines slogging ashore on the beach. Unfortunately, the ships and planes weren't using armor-piercing rounds and the constant firing did little initially to soften the Japanese defenses. The mistakes mounted on the first day. In addition to inflicting little harm on the defending forces, U.S. ships in the area ended their bombing more than 20-minutes early. This gave the Japanese an opportunity to regroup and prepare for the Marines who were still a great distance away from their targets. Air support ended because concerns arose that friendly fire could kill scores of Marines still trying to get over the seawall.

The Japanese forces held their positions and halted the progress of invading U.S. Marines. The Americans were cut-off from reinforcements or fresh supplies. The soldiers trapped on that tiny beachhead were forced to rummage among the dead for hours, trying to find unused water and ammunition that would last until support finally arrived.

Reports from the battlefield were gruesome. Robert Sherrod, a reporter who went ashore with the fifth wave wrote, "It was a ghastly, yet splendid picture, and no man who ever saw it will ever forget. This is the reason Tarawa may truly be called a victory of the spirit: many were killed but more came on."

The battle for Tarawa began in November of 1943, lasting for several bloody days. More than 990 U.S. Marines died during the siege and an additional 2,296 were wounded. The Japanese casualties were staggering. More than 4,690 of their troops were killed. Nearly 200 ships and 900 planes launched from aircraft carriers supported the invasion. The flotilla had been bombing Japanese targets all along the Gilbert and Marshall Islands to the north, preventing aid from arriving for the forces on Tarawa. These ships and aircraft suffered significant losses as well — a total that would mirror that of the battle on land.

The full engagement was so gruesome that U.S. survivors were taken to Hawaii for "R&R" afterwards, which broke existing military protocol. But before slipping off to paradise, the ships carrying surviving soldiers had to navigate waters filled with debris and bodies leftover from the battle.

It is difficult to truly know where my grandfather's service fell in the timeline of the Tarawa battle because he shared almost no details at all. He once mentioned being "volunteered" to go ashore to establish radio communications for the arriving Marines. According to his story, my grandfather — a radio operator on B2 Bombers — was flown in with a small crew to begin the arduous work. This was one of the most horrific battles in Marine history and my grandfather's depiction of his service was limited to a tale of drawing the short straw for an assignment.

He did admit that establishing the radio link took hours because a rain of Japanese bullets kept his small crew pinned down. They finished the assignment and were finally relieved of duty on the island. I suspect they left satisfied, having enabled their comrades' assault on Tarawa. But we'll never know because he didn't share much more than these few details. Most of my information regarding George's role in the battle came from a citation that accompanied his Bronze Star Medal.

According to a letter from Admiral C.W. Nimitz, Staff Sergeant George J. Holahan of the United States Marine Corps Reserve received the Bronze Star Medal, "For meritorious conduct while serving with a Marine Transport Squadron at Tarawa, Gilbert Islands, on November 26, 1943. Having been accepted as a volunteer, he exposed himself to continual enemy sniping for two hours as he worked to assemble the first advanced aircraft radio ground station to be placed in operation in the Gilbert Islands. The task required skill and patience in an area, which offered not the slightest cover from the enemy in pillboxes and log dugouts who were firing wildly in a final show of stubborn resistance. His courage, devotion to duty, and defiance of danger were in keeping with the highest traditions of the United States Naval Service," and I would add, the Greatest Generation.

My grandfather served a few more years before being honorably discharged on November 12, 1945. Very few additional details exist from those remaining years in the service, which seems by my grandfather's design. And it is certainly in keeping with the traditions of warrior heroes from World War II.

George returned to Rochester when he left the Marines and rejoined the Coca-Cola Company. Shortly thereafter, he married Rita Mae McCulloch on June 15, 1946. George and Rita moved in with the McCulloch patriarchs, Frederick and Alice. And their first daughter Karon (my mother) was born a year later on July 16, 1947.

The Holahans are a prime example of the lives led by American families after the war. George left Coke to start a job as a film processor for the Eastman Kodak Company. He would tend bar at the family restaurant, McCulloch's, on weekends and holidays. And he spent free time at the local church men's club.

Times remained tough for American families who were home from the frontlines, as World War II ground to its conclusion. Families were forced to ration their food and supplies. My grandmother Rita used to tell stories of trading silk stocking rations for extra cigarettes and daily household items.

George was the sun in his family's universe, serving as the moral compass and driver of most household activity. He minded all the nieces and nephews and took his mother-in-law to church every Sunday. George did it even though these duties cut into his time teaching my mother how to water ski.

My grandmother took care of her brother following the war, until he was able to care for himself. Butch McCulloch's boat was sunk in a battle in the Pacific. He floated in the water for days, suffering severe shrapnel wounds that left him paralyzed in a Geneva, New York, veteran's hospital. His doctors gave little hope that walking would ever be in Butch's future. Yet Rita regularly traveled the 45-minutes each way to see her brother and to help him regain the full use of his legs.

Butch showed the unending grit and determination characteristic of the Greatest Generation and, ultimately, learned to walk again. But before conquering this infirmity the hospital staff believed he would remain paralyzed. As a result, the doctors decided not to put Butch on a physical therapy program to help him recover. But Rita and Butch were determined and took matters into their own hands. She would help him out of bed, encouraging and supporting him to walk with the assistance of chairs and other furniture around the hospital. At first, Butch was only able to drag himself across the room and down hallways. But the love of a sister and determination of a soldier prevailed, and Butch walked again. And after numerous surgeries, Butch would even play golf into his golden years.

George also exemplified another characteristic of members of the Greatest Generation: he was frugal and protective of family resources, unwilling to risk losing them. That's really an interesting juxtaposition considering that he and countless other soldiers were so brave and daring on the battlefields of World War II. For instance, a few of George's in-laws purchased early shares of stock in Haloid, a local Rochester company. Nobody in George's family could convince him to risk the family's money on speculation. It didn't matter that the stock showed great promise. Haloid would eventually be known around the world as Xerox, making millions for many early stockholders.

I suspect your family experience mirrors the details of mine outlined above. I could go on describing my family but there's no need because we all know a George Holahan or Butch McCulloch. In fact, they were probably just like your father, uncle or grandfather.

These men were more than soldiers and heroes. Together, the Greatest Generation formed a backbone and foundation for a nation that would flourish in the 1950s once the global battles of World War

II were nothing more than echoes in our history books. The characteristics outlined in this chapter were seemingly universal among the generation tested by the fires of depression and war: integrity, stoicism, devotion to family, hard work and civic-mindedness.

Amazingly, rhetoric and controversy has recently bubbled to the surface in regards to the "true status" of the Greatest Generation. Some question whether the WWII Memorial deserved prominent Washington Mall placement or if the generation's actions really warranted the lofty moniker bestowed upon them by Tom Brokaw. And these critics question Hollywood's glorification of the generation's role in world politics through movies like *Saving Private Ryan*.

There are apparently individuals who believe the "Greatest Generation" is nothing but great big hype. A vocal group of critics contend that the survivors of the Great Depression and battlers of world tyranny were almost as much to blame for the hostile global environment as the "enemy" they fought. To some, primarily citizens in parts of Europe, Japan and other Pacific Rim nations, the United States represented an evil force that destroyed lives and committed unspeakable crimes against humanity.

A book deconstructing the debate over the Greatest Generation would make for interesting reading. And several very good attempts already exist. But that's not the purpose of this text. Instead, let's turn to the undisputable facts and characteristics of the Greatest Generation.

There is no disputing that the Greatest Generation was forged by the grit and steel of the Industrial Revolution. And as a group, they endured some of the most daunting challenges in American history. Not only did they survive these tests, but America prospered because of their hard work and sacrifice. The world became safer when the war ended even though nations were dividing into Cold War camps.

The Greatest Generation drove the global economy's transformation from the Industrial Age to consumer production. World War II created increased production capacity within the world's leading man-ufacturers. And these companies took advantage of that momentum, retooling their bullet, boat and bomb factories into production of more consumer-oriented goods. The technological innovation that helped to end the war led to progress in TVs, refrigerators and automobiles.

Not only were the accomplishments of this generation great but the manner in which they went about their daily lives was an example for each of us. And perhaps most germane to this book, members of the Greatest Generation set an exceedingly high civic bar. Throughout their lives, they engaged in churches, communities and families. They were active members of local Rotary, the Masons, Moose Lodge, Knights of Columbus, chambers of commerce and other social and civic groups. And they voted — consistently! As we'll see shortly, this dedication is a direct result of the difficult times overcome by the gen-eration and their service in the war.

This first section of the book will define the Greatest Generation, what they accomplished and why they are the civic standard for our nation. We've evolved as both a nation and global community since the early to mid-1900s. But the course plotted and example set by America's Greatest Generation is important to understand and emu-late. We begin by examining the best examples of participation, in the hopes of calling all Americans to action that lives up to the legacy of the Greatest Generation.

Chapter 2

Who Is the Greatest Generation?

The amazing thing about the moniker, "Greatest Generation," is that very little definition or context was required for people to understand who Tom Brokaw was talking about when he coined the term in his best-selling book by the same name. People understood that he was referring to what most experts call the G.I. Generation, those American men and women born between 1911 and 1924. However, the term Greatest Generation is often expanded to include additional Americans born between 1901 and 1910, which is traditionally known as the Interbellum Generation.

Developing a definition for this generation is critical to truly understanding why they've played such a pivotal role in shaping American society and, frankly, the history of the world. The Greatest Generation can be divided into two segments. The first is the Interbellum Generation, born during the first decade of the 20th century. They were too young to fight in World War I and were typically too old for active service by the time World War II broke out.

Members of this group were shaped by significant events during their formative years. Namely, they experienced the Roaring '20s and the Great Depression first hand. And they arrived at adulthood before Franklin Delano Roosevelt was elected president, introducing New Deal policies that altered the way most Americans viewed government. The majority of these early experiences helped to form a liberal political ideology that created programs and policies that would shape America's future, particularly around economic issues. This generational segment's political beliefs were embodied by President Lyndon Johnson's administration.

The second segment of the Greatest Generation is typically credited with fighting and winning World War II. While they experienced portions of the Roaring '20s and Great Depression, they were too young to truly comprehend the political and social landscape at that time. Upon returning home from the war, this cohort would be mostly responsible for the rapid economic growth of America's economy and the overwhelming sense of traditional family values that resulted. In essence, they would become the establishment, enduring the first significant generation gap in American history with their Baby Boomer children.

The common definition for a generation gap is a "vast difference in cultural norms between a younger generation and their elders." The term was first widely used in Western countries during the 1960s to account for the cultural differences between members of the Greatest Generation and their Baby Boomer children. Differences have always existed between generations, no matter the culture. But during the '60s, when Baby Boomers came of age, the generational differences were more pronounced than at any other time. America took on a palpably different feel in the 1960s as musical tastes, hair and clothing styles, attitudes toward drugs and political beliefs ranged far and wide. Some credit the sheer size of the Baby Boomer generation with the extreme cultural shift, perhaps in large measure because of the power and influence they felt from their numbers.

A good example of these cultural differences was the popular music of that time. Young people were listening to rock and soul music that was far different from Bing Crosby, Doris Day and the big bands favored by their parents. Hairstyles and clothing also presented differences. Gone were the days of crew cuts and flattops for men. Instead, many grew out their hair as a symbol of rebellion against parental control, or as an expression of dropping out of mainstream culture.

Yet perhaps the greatest cultural clash centered on the Vietnam War. Young people protested on college campuses across the nation, which was in stark contrast to the universal national support for World War II by their parents. And the protest culture was fueled in large measure by sex and drugs, which were counter to the traditional mores the Greatest Generation established upon their return from foreign fields of battle. While these differences were not adopted by every member of the Baby Boomer generation, enough did to create near-violent clashes in countless American families.

The above information is important background about the Greatest Generation, but they can truly be summed up in a handful of characteristics that ran as a strong generational current across America. It would be easy to simply call them role models, but such a banal term would cheapen their legacy. These were people who endured unthinkable economic hardship during the Great Depression, foiled the Nazis and socialism during World War II, built a great American economic engine and established bedrock cultural mores and family norms upon their return. These experiences combined to create a set of characteristics that are missing on a lot of levels in American society today: dogged persistence, heroism, self-sacrifice, family cohesion and valuing team bonding over individual accolades.

Resilience: Staying the Course and Bouncing Back

Members of the Greatest Generation set a remarkable example of what it means to endure tragedy and hardship. Doing so with grace and overcoming obstacles because of a can-do attitude was based on perseverance and hard work. Just think about the fires this generation walked through. The Great Depression fundamentally changed American culture.

Families were displaced from homes that had been in their possesssion for generations. Many of the unemployed and destitute moved into large shanty towns built of driftwood and found their meals in soup kitchens and bread lines. It is hard to imagine the humility created by waiting for a handout, instead of working hard to earn their keep. Americans living at that time went from the security of a roaring economy to one where earning even a few dollars a week for the most basic of necessities seemed so far out of reach.

World War II also created a selflessness that was the result of being part of something bigger than oneself. Serving alongside some 16 million American soldiers in battlefields and ocean fronts around the world taught members of the Greatest Generation to rely on one another. They also grew to appreciate simply doing one's job and being lucky enough to survive another day.

Think about the Battle of Tarawa Island outlined at the start of this section. Hundreds of Marines died on the beaches and in the bloody jungles of that Pacific island in less than 72 hours. And the surviving soldiers packed up their gear, hopped back on their ships and went off to the next battle.

The soldiers of World War II saw carnage — some 300,000 members of the G.I. Generation died and another 670,000 were wounded — yet they persevered to win a war against tyranny and evil. And life at home was no picnic for most Americans either. The families of our soldiers endured rationing of the most basic necessities, like food and gasoline. Their daily sustenance was willingly tied to the fate of the American war machine. Companies were focused on making parts for war — bullets, boats, planes and weapons — instead of luxury items or even the most basic necessities we associate with a free society. Yet Americans survived and persevered, sacrificing to ensure that our military had the necessary tools for victory.

Making the Extraordinary, Ordinary

The events of September 11th reawakened our worship of modern heroes. As a result of the blind commitment to their job, which led to the loss of hundreds of lives, firefighters, policeman and other emergency workers again became the idols of American youth. Costume companies and shops couldn't keep up with the demand for emergency worker outfits for Halloween 2001. Children everywhere began to dream again about being a hero — someone who gave of him or herself for the betterment and safety of others. Oliver Stone brought home this sense of selfless commitment to others in his stunning movie, *Twin Towers* in 2006.

Yet before 9/11, it was hard to identify heroes in America. Hollywood tried, but their versions tended to be crusaders in some far-off, futuristic, technology-driven world. Think of Keanu Reeves in *The Matrix* or Will Smith in *Men in Black*. Both fought to save humanity, but in worlds that looked far different than ours.

The Greatest Generation didn't have to look too far for heroes. They had countless examples of people doing the extraordinary all around them — even before engaging in battles that would decide the fate of the world. Numerous examples exist, but let's focus on some of the most celebrated:

- Charles Lindbergh not only captured the imagination of Americans, he inspired people the world over. Lindbergh left Roosevelt Field outside New York City in his *Spirit of St. Louis* plane on the morning of May 20, 1927. His mission was clear: to be the first in history to fly solo across the Atlantic Ocean. Few events in history have captivated the nation like Lindbergh's flight. People sat glued to their radios, listening for news of the flight and reports of his safe landing. In the end, some 100,000 people came out to Le Bourget Field in France to greet Lindbergh and to celebrate his amazing feat.
- In sports, we had the famous "Joe's" — Louis and DiMaggio. Louis was a legend almost from the moment he came out swinging from his corner in 1934. He had style and skills unmatched or even seen in the boxing world at that time. He quickly rose through the ranks and took part in some of the most memorable bouts in boxing history, including a slugfest with Primo Carnera in front of 62,000 fans at Yankee Stadium and his destruction of Max Schmeling in 1938, the only man to have knocked Louis out up to that point. The Schmeling fight was more than just a sporting event. It had a global psychological impact because a black American athlete beat Germany's sports icon — throwing a body blow to Hitler's ideological ruminations.

DiMaggio, the Yankee Clipper, was more than just a baseball player. He was the greatest player on the greatest team of all time and a symbol of how hard work can combine with opportunity to produce greatness. He was also a cultural icon, as evidenced by his marriage to Marilyn Monroe, America's favorite movie star. On many levels, DiMaggio *was* the American dream. He was part of an Italian immigrant family struggling to get by in New York City. He grew from a shy boy to a humble giant, and became known as the "Greatest American Icon" and "The Last American Hero." This last moniker led Simon & Garfunkel to ask, "Where have you gone Joe DiMaggio, our nation turns its lonely eyes to you?" This was their lament about how America had drifted in the '60s from a global, moral authority united in a vision of the world — to one divided over Vietnam and the need for war.

These examples provided a clear image of heroism in all its forms to members of the Greatest Generation. These portraits of courage made it clear that heroism was not necessarily something to aspire to or brag about. Rather, Lindbergh, Louis, DiMaggio and others showed that difficult situations were something to rise to and conquer. And these legends did so with humility and a lack of braggadocio. Obviously, this attitude is missing in today's world of end-zone dances, over-the-top home-run trots and in-your-face celebrations. Not to mention, constant reports of athletes using steroids and other performance-enhancing substances to cheat the system and beat the competition. For the Greatest Generation, the extraordinary was ordinary — just a part of everyday life.

Family Unity

Family was the cornerstone of life for members of the Greatest Generation. They relied upon each other to survive the Depression, a war-torn world and other forces ripping the fabric of their daily lives. Families at the time were large, often living under one roof and they stayed together through difficult times.

That's quite a departure from the world today, where nearly two-thirds of all marriages end in divorce. And according to author Jennifer Marshall in a 2003 article, "Current trends indicate that by the year 2015, one of every two American babies will be born to a single mother, and illegitimacy will surpass divorce as the main cause of fatherlessness." For members of the Greatest Generation, marriage was a lifelong bond and prerequisite for childbirth. These notions are largely gone today, replaced by the idea that "it takes a village" to raise a child. That's not to say Americans don't understand the value of family and staying together. It's just that so many factors combined to replace the characteristics and commitment to unity shown by members of the Greatest Generation.

No "I" in Team

America today is a place where the letter "I" is prominently fixed in our collective vision of the world. Instead of playing outside with children in the neighborhood, many American kids spend hours online alone, playing video games or surfing the net. Instead of working for a company as part of a team, people are increasingly doing their jobs from the comfort of home, telecommuting and removing the bonds of groups in corporate America.

These are just two examples of how different life is from the days when the Greatest Generation led America. Perhaps that generation's commitment to team and service is best summed by author and historian Stephen Ambrose, who said they had a "strong commitment to community, service and teamwork." All of the major experiences endured by this generation led them to rely upon others for the most basic of necessities.

In World War II, soldiers lived and died next to their best friends, building a bond and purpose that was far greater than the individual.

This attitude, shaped and hardened by economic turmoil and war, became a core principal of life — success was possible when individuals worked together. Hard work was also a core value developed through the trying times of depression and war. For most, the ideas of teams and hard work were inexplicably linked (these ideas will be studied in detail in chapter three). For the Greatest Generation, the solutions were as large as the problems they sought to remedy.

And all were accomplished as a team — as a nation.

Chapter 3

The Greatest Accomplishments of a Generation

The previous chapter outlined the core values that defined the Greatest Generation. In this chapter, we seek to provide snapshots or vignettes of the achievements produced by those principles. As outlined in the previous section, the solutions offered by the Greatest Generation were as complex and multilayered as the challenges they sought to remedy. And every obstacle was traversed as a team, with a plan and a can-do spirit.

The WPA

The Works Progress Administration (WPA) was perhaps the first example of the Greatest Generation's belief in large-scale teamwork as the tool for overcoming hardship. President Franklin D. Roosevelt created the WPA in 1935 through executive order as part of his New

Deal. The program was altered in 1939 when it was transferred to the Federal Works Agency.

The WPA sought to reshape America by paying the unemployed for hard work on an array of grand projects. Congress took unprecedented action, appropriating nearly $5 trillion dollars to fund the program. The WPA provided the unemployed with jobs and led to the completion of diverse projects, including highways, building construction, slum clearance and reforestation.

The program was so grand that it was rife with confusion, waste and politics. Yet it was visionary and grand in scope, and is credited with stimulating private business during the depression years. It also supported state efforts to complete programs and projects they were previously unable to fund. Perhaps more importantly, the WPA restored hope, trust and faith in government and the world. And best of all, it was predicated on hard work. Jobs replaced handouts, and America began to recover and prosper as a result.

But Roosevelt and the New Dealers wanted the program to be more than just building and infrastructure improvements. The WPA utilized the unique tools and skills of unemployed Americans from all walks of life to bring about a cultural revolution of sorts as well. For instance, people with literary skills were supported by the Federal Writers' Project, which prepared state and regional guidebooks, organized archives, indexed newspapers and conducted sociological and historical studies.

Artists were also supported. The Federal Arts Project provided unemployed artists with opportunities to use their skills for the beautification of America. Murals, sculptures and other public art were created to decorate post offices, schools and numerous other buildings and spaces. Musicians also participated, organizing symphonies, orchestras and community vocal programs. And the Federal Theatre Project entertained a nation by writing musical scores and plays that were unique in their experimentation with new forms. Actors also toured the country, performing old and new plays and introducing the art form to communities that had been previously unexposed.

By March 1936, more than 3.4 million Americans had participated in WPA programming. The WPA program closed its doors on June 30, 1943, marking the end of one of the most expansive social engineering programs in world history. In the end, the WPA had employed more than 8.5 million individuals and completed nearly 1.5 million projects. The hard work of formerly unemployed and hopeless Americans built more than 651,087 miles of highways, roads and streets. And they also constructed or repaired nearly 124,031 bridges; 125,110 public buildings; 8,192 parks; and 853 airport landing fields.

World War II

As covered in countless books, articles, movies, TV shows, etc., fighting World War II was perhaps the most significant undertaking of that generation. Many claim that the Greatest Generation simply saved the world. By the end of World War II, more than 16 million Americans had served in the armed forces, and more than 400,000 of those had died. The political and physical landscapes of Europe, the Pacific and much of the world were changed — as was American culture.

While a momentous achievement, we will leave in-depth analysis of World War II to experts in other areas. We all know the stories of courage, honor and teamwork that resulted from this global conflict. Instead, I prefer using this chapter to highlight perhaps one of the most important, yet most overlooked outcomes of World War II — the changing role of women in American society. This was perhaps the most notable cultural shift during World War II. Until America entered the war, women traditionally played the role of mother and homemaker, serving as the cornerstone of daily family life. But that changed as men went overseas to fight and women were needed to fill the void.

Women like "Rosie the Riveter," who built planes, made ammunition and produced the basic necessities for soldiers on the war front, and nurses on the battlefield and women who assumed the daily jobs of men fighting overseas changed the workforce forever. Women not only became an indispensable part of the war effort, they became a necessity for the expanding economy afterwards as well. Many women returned to their traditional role as family leader, yet thousands of others continued to work due to financial need or the availability of jobs following the war. In stark contrast to the days prior to World War II, the 1950s saw only five men in the workforce for every two women.

Waging and winning World War II took the strength, courage and determination of an entire generation — its men *and* women. While perhaps its biggest accomplishment, triumphing against tyranny was just one of many for this generation. Their impact and leadership continued for decades after the war.

The 1950s

Life after World War II was supposed to usher in a return to "normalcy" for Americans. While daily life tended to find a routine, it was much different than before the war. The 1950s are often referred to as the "Golden Age" because of the economic expansion and the rise of consumerism and stability derived from the creation of the nuclear family. The expanding role of television also propelled the Golden Age forward. President Harry Truman launched transcontinental television transmission with a speech in 1951. In a very short time, TV would become the dominant mass medium, changing America's cultural landscape forever.

For instance, in the early '50s, young people watched TV for more hours than they went to school. TV became part of daily life, and Americans began to define themselves by the people and experiences they watched onscreen. Programs like *You Are There* made historical events real for people in a way that wasn't possible before. The show allowed them to become "eye witnesses" to the world not just in front of them, but around the globe. Americans, especially those living in rural areas, began to feel less isolated from their fellow citizens as the world came to the family living room.

The factories that fueled the American war machine now had excess capacity and turned their focus to the goods of a consumer economy — fueling a new era of production and economic development. As a result, unemployment was low, and soldiers took advantage of the G.I. Bill, which finally made college possible for thousands of veterans. The average annual salary was $2,992 and a loaf of bread cost 14¢. More than 6.5 million cars were on the road, taking people across newly-created highways to their homes in the suburbs. Wealth created through this economic expansion allowed Americans to buy luxury goods like TVs, clothes and single-family dwellings. And the ranch style home of the suburbs was born.

Education also fundamentally changed forever during this time. In 1954, America's educational "separate but equal" policy was overturned by the U.S. Supreme Court. The court, led by Chief Justice Earl Warren, found in *Brown v. the Board of Education of Topeka, Kansas* that, under the Constitution, separate facilities for blacks did not automatically create equal opportunities. The decision set off a slow but powerful chain reaction as evidenced by African-American female Autherine J. Lucy's successfully enrolling in the University of Alabama at Tuscaloosa in 1956.

Integration of public schools began to take place quietly across America. But the issue came to a head publicly in 1957, when the first black teenager enrolled in the then all-white Little Rock Central High School. The resulting battle in Little Rock showed that public opinion on this issue was deeply divided and would continue to rage into the 1960s.

World War II ended, but global uncertainty continued as nations chose sides in the increasingly frigid Cold War. President Truman authorized production of the hydrogen bomb and committed American troops to Korea. And the impact of the Cold War was felt deeply in America. Conservatism and anticommunist feelings ran throughout much of American society. This new attitude was perhaps best symbolized by the addition of the phrase "under God" to the Pledge of Allegiance. For many Americans, religious fervor was akin to a deep expression of their repulsion of communism.

Members of the Greatest Generation defined the 1950s. This is evident in the expansion of consumerism, due largely to the television advertising model, the emphasis on family values, the explosion of technology and a steely resistance to communism. Members of the Greatest Generation left their fingerprints on every aspect of life in the "Golden Age."

The 1960s

Chapter Two of this section foreshadows the fact that the 1960s were perhaps the last big gasp for the Greatest Generation. By decade's end, they held little political power or significant influence over American culture and society. Their Baby Boomer children redefined America by protesting the war in Vietnam and changing cultural norms with their use of drugs and the rise and spread of "free love."

During the '60s, America's population grew by more than 22 million people. The average annual salary was $4,743 and teachers earned an average of $5,174. Minimum hourly wage was $1.

Let's not completely write off the Greatest Generation and their influence during the 1960s. They are credited with a number of important accomplishments during the 1960s, even as their conservative influence and power waned. Perhaps their birthing the enormous population of young people who took the reins of power in the 1960s is chief among the generations continuing influences. Nearly 70 million children of the Greatest Generation became teenagers and young adults in this decade. The Baby Boomers redefined every element of American life. The fads and fashions, music and literature of the 1960s all bore the Baby Boomer stamp.

It was clear though, that the Greatest Generation wasn't quite ready to give up full control of government and power. In fact, the generation's leaders attempted to conquer a new set of challenges that sprang up during the 1950s. Leaders from the Greatest Generation set out to tackle the War on Poverty, the conflict in Vietnam, Civil Rights and launched the space race. Perhaps most importantly, the eventual defeat of communism was sown in the seeds planted by leaders from the Greatest Generation.

President Johnson's War on Poverty

The War on Poverty was yet another example of the Greatest Generation's belief that big problems required big, government-driven solutions. President Lyndon Johnson, announced his plan to attack American poverty in his 1964 State of the Union Address. He called the program "A Nationwide War on the Sources of Poverty."

Outlining his bold vision, President Johnson told Congress that "because it is right, because it is wise, and because, for the first time in our history, it is possible to conquer poverty, I submit, for the consideration of the Congress and the country, the Economic Opportunity Act of 1964." The plan did not merely build upon existing governmental frameworks and funding programs. As Johnson put it, his legislation charted "a new course" by not merely putting a Band-Aid on the results of poverty, but by attacking it at its causes. The plan consisted of five main themes/elements:

- Provide nearly half a million underprivileged young Americans an opportunity to learn skills, continue their education and find useful work.
- Provide every American community the opportunity to develop comprehensive plans to battle poverty locally, with assistance from Washington to implement them.
- Provide opportunities for Americans to enlist as volunteers in the War Against Poverty.
- Provide farmers and workers the chance to break through barriers that prevent their escape from poverty.
- Provide a federal bureaucracy, the Office of Economic Opportunity that organizes the national battle in one central location.

Specifically, the War on Poverty consisted of programs to help those Americans who were not trained for a trade, or lacked the education to succeed in a modern marketplace. This component of the program had three elements: A new Job Corps program that was built on the WPA model and would enlist and train 100,000 men; a new Work-Training Program managed by the Department of Labor that was to provide nearly 200,000 men and women between the ages of

16 and 21 the skills for lifelong work; and a new national Work-Study Program run by the Department of Health, Education and Welfare that allocated federal funds to support 140,000 part-time jobs for young Americans who weren't going to college for financial reasons.

President Johnson's War on Poverty also sought to "strike poverty at its source" through the Community Action program that asked local communities to develop their own plans for tackling the issue. Local volunteers were to be recruited because "thousands of Americans have volunteered to serve the needs of other lands. Thousands more want the chance to serve the needs of their own land." And the program sought to: root out poverty by providing loans and guarantees as incentives for businesses to offer jobs to the unemployed; offer retraining programs for out-of-work parents; help farmers with land purchases; and other efforts.

Many of President Johnson's weapons used during the war on poverty still exist today, in programs like Medicaid, Medicare and Head Start. Like many leaders from the Greatest Generation, Johnson saw an America in need and plotted a course of aid. The vision was grand, as were the tools aimed to bring about results. Other scholars can argue the program's successes and failures. But for purposes of this book, the lessons are clear. When confronted by a problem, the Greatest Generation organized a response plan, boldly called their team to action and mobilized tremendous resources to ensure victory.

Chapter 4

The Greatest Civic Participation — Ever!

The concept of social capital will be explored in detail in future chapters of this book. For now, it is important to know that a community's social capital is directly tied to its rates of civic participation. The three main ingredients of social capital are political involvement, community engagement and social trust. Reviewing the rates of social capital among the Greatest Generation shows that they are the most engaged in American history.

The term social trust is derived from combining trust in a range of groups, including neighbors, friends, store employees and other local figures. It also includes trust among different genders, races and interest groups. The implication is that communities are weaker when there is low social trust. For instance, people are less likely to ask for and provide help to people in their community if trust is low.

Generalized trust has evaporated over the years, especially as the Greatest Generation lost influence in society. In the 1960s, at the zenith of their influence, nearly 55 percent of American adults believed others in the community could be trusted most or all of the time. By comparison, only 30 percent of adults felt the same way in 1998.

The 1998 statistics are a red flag for the future of American civic participation unless things change drastically, particularly because youth were by far the least trusting group surveyed.

Trust in government is also an important factor in the health of communities. During the reign of the Greatest Generation, more people trusted government to do the right thing than they do today. As we'll see in subsequent chapters, that change is due in large part to Vietnam, Watergate and the more personal, but no-less-damaging scandals like those endured during the Clinton years.

In the 1960 survey, nearly 75 percent of Americans trusted government to do the right thing most or all of the time. In stark contrast are the results of the 1998 survey where less than 25 percent trusted government to do the right thing all or most of the time. Overall, the loss of trust in government and individuals has significant ramifications for our future, as less-trusting people will be less inclined to work with government or others in their communities to tackle important issues.

Community involvement was also a hallmark of the Greatest Generation. Again, many of this group's early life experiences required cooperating with friends and family to survive the difficult tasks that lay ahead. And as a result, they believed in community and worked hard to build it.

Community engagement is defined in numerous ways, from volunteering time to donating money to charities. The Greatest Generation set the bar high on all fronts. In terms of financial donations, the share of government funds that went to charities nearly doubled from 1929 through 1964, at a time when members of this generation held sway over the purse strings of government. And the total contributed rose continuously from year-to-year during that span. In stark contrast is the importance government has placed on charitable giving as younger generations have risen to power. Charitable funding has dropped significantly, lowering by more than a third today, to approximately 1940 levels. While government has shifted funding priorities and institutionalized some of this giving over time (Head Start, Medicaid, etc.), the overall assistance levels have nonetheless fallen-off dramatically.

Rates of volunteering have fallen off for the Greatest Generation as they move into their senior years. Obviously, health and the ability to actively serve others diminish as seniors age. Yet the level of service provided throughout their lives has been unparalleled, which is a cornerstone of their commitment to community and service to others. The numbers and depth of this engagement will be revisited in future sections of this book.

Finally, the Greatest Generation was more involved in the political and electoral process than any other generation in American history. From 1972 to the present, members of this generation have accounted for the largest segment of voter participation, election after election. The group has been tremendously active in Washington, D.C., and the result has been significant political power and an ability to define the policy landscape in local governments and state capitals across the country. This idea, too, will be discussed in detail later in the book.

But you only need to take a look at the issues being discussed in the halls of government today to clearly see the power of this group. Congress battles over Social Security, Medicaid and prescription drug benefits everyday, issues that matter most directly to our elderly. Seniors possesss such amazing power because, as the rhetorical rule of thumb states, "80 percent of 80-year-olds vote, while only 20 percent of 20-year-olds cast ballots!"

Let's turn to the facts. In 1972, members of the Greatest Generation accounted for nearly 50 percent of U.S. voter turnout. Their numbers are in stark contrast to 18- to 20-year-olds, of whom only 40 percent went to the polls, accounting for slightly more than 6 percent of the electorate. And keep in mind that 1972 was the first election in which 18-year-olds had the right to vote, which should have elevated enthusiasm.

It is important to understand just how much the Greatest Generation has meant to America and the world. They have been a stabilizing force in a tempest of chaos. They battled through the Great Depression, only to prosper in times of global peril. They were called to fight in World War II, and sacrificed mightily to bring an end to the run of terror led by Hitler and the original "Axis of Evil." And they came home from war to preside over one of the most ideal times in American history — the Golden Age of consumerism and family values.

They set an example that should guide our efforts if we are to tackle the issues facing the world today. In their modest manner, members of the Greatest Generation provided a road map for building a safer, more prosperous and involved world. To make the world a more secure and prosperous place today, we must be dedicated to the cause and persevere at all costs; we must rise to the occasion; we must make the extraordinary ordinary; we must keep our families strong; and we must work as a team.

Section II

Chapters 5 – 8

The Genesis of American Cynicism: The Detrimental Role of War, Scandal and Media

Chapter 5

Introduction

Individuals seeking to explain America's disinterest in the civic process often blame a apathy that evolved from an even more entrenched cynicism that ripples through all walks of life across the country. It's as if these two words somehow make diminishing levels of participation understandable, or worse, acceptable. "Cynicism" and "apathy" have become shorthand for American distrust of the political process and governmental institutions.

As will become clear in the following chapters, civic cynicism and apathy took root in the American psyche during the 1960s and 1970s when the nation was sharply divided over the Vietnam War and when former President Richard Nixon put an American face on political power run amok. These fears were reinforced in the following two decades by the Iran-Contra scandal and the Clinton impeachment. And as will be discussed, the media have played a prominent role in the growing American cynicism.

This powerful current of distrust is an important factor in America's civic decline that has strengthened over time. But it is one of many that coalesce to create a series of barriers to participation. The following section examines the impact the Vietnam War, Watergate and media have had on American civic life and attempts to prove that there is a direct correlation between political scandal and decreased trust and civic participation.

The problem is real and dangerous: distrust of government, elected officials and our public institutions is at an all-time high. Yet using cynicism and apathy to justify our ailing civic process, without pointing to the historical factors that led to these pervasive feelings, exacerbates the problem. And in fact, ignoring the roots of our cynicism is in short, apathetic and cynical.

Prior to Vietnam, Americans believed that government and its leaders could be trusted to do the right thing. Surveys in 1958 and 1964 found that three-quarters of Americans trusted leaders in Washington to do the right thing. But that public support quickly faded in 1965. Government began to falter under the growing protests around the Vietnam War and Civil Rights issues. As a result, only 65 percent of Americans trusted government in 1966, 61 percent in 1968 and an astonishingly low 53 percent in 1970. Reflect for a moment on that sharp decline: In less than six years, public trust of government institutions and leaders dropped more than 20 percent!

Watergate and the subsequent and related scandals sustained the declining levels of trust. By 1974, only 36 percent of Americans trusted government, and in the years since, government has accomplished little to shake Americans of that distrust. President Reagan's optimism and the economic boom of the 1980s rallied trust a little, raising it to 44 percent in 1984. But confidence levels quickly dropped again during the Gulf War and the Clinton years.

Statistically speaking, voter turnout levels, which will be discussed at length throughout this book, closely parallel America's degree of faith in government. The presidential elections of 1972 witnessed the lowest turnout in decades, with a mere 55 percent of eligible Americans casting a ballot. Turnout of 55 percent today would be welcomed. But turnout in 1972 was down from nearly 61 percent in 1968, less than 62 percent in 1964 and 63 percent in 1960. The trend continued with the 1974 midterm elections, as 44.7 percent of voters went to the polls. And voter numbers continued to drop for decades, reversing momentarily in 1992 with the election of Bill Clinton. We will discuss the impact of outreach to young Americans and hope spurred by candidate Clinton in later sections of this book.

Hopefully by the end of this section, it will be clear that, while pervasive and deep-rooted, cynicism and apathy are not acceptable excuses for diminished participation. The attitudes are not inherent in every American. Nor are they insurmountable. The basic steps for action, and the principles of good citizenship outlined in subsequent sections can overcome these barriers.

Chapter 6

The Vietnam War Shakes America's Trust in Government and Politicians

The previous section of this book painted a prosperous, optimistic and unified picture of American life in the 1950s. This lifestyle continued into the mid-1960s until Vietnam took hold of American culture and threatened to tear the nation apart at the seams. The growing dissent over Vietnam manifested into a great generational, race and class divide reinforced by changing cultural norms related to music, fashion, political discourse, drug use and sexual experimentation. The roots of modern apathy were sewn in large measure by Vietnam, resulting in a visceral cynicism toward America's government institutions and leaders.

As outlined previously, voter participation also began to decline as entire segments of citizens "dropped out" of the system. Dr. Timothy Leary — noted LSD proponent and philosopher — coined a popular phrase that came to signify the generation: "turn on, tune in, drop out." Examining the events surrounding Vietnam will help us better understand why such a dramatic rift in American society was created at the time. The following is not intended to be an exhaustive history of the Vietnam War because its roots and rationale span decades and are too tangled to unravel in a book about civic participation (it's not even universally discussed in American high schools today). But context for the war and resulting protests are important for the sake of understanding where today's rampant cynicism first took hold.

The United States was involved in Vietnam for decades before engaging in open conflict during the 1960s. In 1954, a multinational conference including France, the United States, Cambodia, the Democratic Republic of Vietnam, Laos, the People's Republic of China, the State of Vietnam, the Union of Soviet Socialist Republics and the United Kingdom reached an agreement that set a demilitarized zone under the 17th parallel. The North remained under communist rule and the South was to be led by Prime Minister Ngo Dinh Diem. These newly-divided nations created a fresh battlefront in the Cold War.

In October of 1954, President Dwight Eisenhower pledged his support to Diem's government, committing troops to protect the new regime. The political and physical landscape continued to change in 1955 as the Republic of Vietnam was established in the south, and Diem became president there after defeating Bao Dai in a referendum. This new government put pressure on the North, and fighting broke out within a year. The fighting drew America ever closer to the Vietnam front, with the nation's first two casualties taking place in 1959 during an attack on the Bien Hoa billets.

Widespread American dissent over Vietnam was minimal at this time but would gain steam shortly after President Kennedy was elected in 1960. At the time of his election, there were only 900 military "advisors" in Vietnam, a number that would grow sharply year-to-year. Diem's government was under siege, and he tried securing control in 1959 by creating a law prosecuting all dissidents. The result was increased opposition, which culminated in the creation of the National

Liberation Front — known as the Viet Cong — in 1960. President Kennedy quickly responded by committing more American military troops — in the form of "advisors" — to South Vietnam. He made clear that troops on the ground would only engage if fired upon.

Events in Vietnam quickly spiraled out of control, as did dissent across America. Vice President Lyndon Johnson visited Vietnam in May of 1961 and returned home with a recommendation for increased aid to America's allies in that region. About one month later, President Kennedy met for the first time with Soviet leader Nikita Khrushchev in Vienna. The meeting cemented his belief that Vietnam was likely to become the final front in the escalating war between democracy and communism.

Troop counts rose to slightly more than 3,000, which prompted more forceful and outspoken opposition at home. The events of 1963 rapidly escalated both America's involvement in Vietnam and the protests at home. President Diem increased persecution of opposition elements as he fought to retain control of the new government. The crackdowns were so severe that Buddhist monks staged public displays of disobedience that rocked the psyche of American protestors and government leaders alike. In August of that year, a Buddhist monk immolated himself (covering his body in gasoline and striking a match) on the streets of Phanthiet, 100 miles east of Saigon. This horrific example of the pressure felt by dissidents was a direct assault on the authoritarian regime of President Diem and his family. This was the second such display of unrest and would be followed by three more immolations — the last, an elderly Buddhist nun.

Vietnam continued to unravel throughout the year, but perhaps most violently on November 1st, when a coup led by General Duong Van Minh overthrew the regime. The Kennedy administration, through Ambassador Henry Cabot Lodge, sent messages to Diem prior to the coup stating that they no longer trusted his leadership. The CIA was even aware of the coup in advance and agreed to stay out of the "internal conflict." The dwindling U.S. support and constant threat of coup drove Diem and his brother Ngo Dinh Nhu into hiding, leaving room for Van Minh to take over.

American troops, now totaling more than 16,300 "in country," were increasingly engaged in battles with the Viet Cong. The political rivalries and destabilization of Vietnam that resulted from the ouster of Diem contributed to the problems plaguing the U.S. war effort. The nation's military activity was further hampered by President Kennedy's assassination on November 22, 1963. Ironically, President Kennedy died a mere three weeks after President Diem had been assassinated. President Johnson's transition to power and the resulting instability in our government switched the nation's focus away from activities taking place halfway around the world.

The conflict in Vietnam would take a tumultuous turn in 1964, as American troops officially engaged the North Vietnamese following events in the Gulf of Tonkin. The Gulf lies between the eastern coast of North Vietnam and the western coast of a small island called Hainan. The United States used this area to stage its Seventh Fleet, consisting in part of the destroyers *Maddox* and *C. Turner Joy*, and the *U.S.S. Ticonderoga* (an aircraft carrier). The *Maddox* was conducting surveillance missions in the area on August 2nd in an effort to gather intelligence on North Vietnamese radar and coastal defenses. Specific details of the engagement are still unclear to the public today. However, it is believed that North Vietnamese torpedo patrol boats attacked the *Maddox*, forcing the *U.S.S. Ticonderoga* to unleash its aircraft on the enemy. The superior U.S. force fought off the initial patrols and sank several additional boats in the area.

Congress took action a few days after another purported attack on the *Maddox* and *C. Turner Joy* by the North Vietnamese. On August 7th, both chambers of Congress passed the "Tonkin Gulf Resolution" (by a 416 to 0 vote in the house and 88 to 2 count in the Senate). The resolution authorized President Johnson to "take all necessary measures to repel armed attack against the forces of the United States and to prevent further aggression."

These events led to a significant escalation of U.S. involvement in Vietnam. By July 1965, more than 80,000 U.S. troops were sent to the region, and in April, President Johnson approved plans for the troops to commence offensive operations in North Vietnam for the first time. A proposal sent by President Johnson to leaders in North Vietnam shortly after U.S. forces commenced attacks in the north was immediately rejected. Under the terms of the agreement, America offered to exchange financial aid for peace. Unfortunately this gesture was overlooked by anti-war segments of the American population. And the increased military action led to a swift response by protesters.

On April 17th, Students for a Democratic Society launched the first major anti-war rally in Washington, D.C. Simultaneous protests took place in more than 40 cities across the country on October 15th and 16th. These events were followed by the first major military engagement between the United States and North Vietnam in November.

The conflict and anti-war protests both hit a fever pitch in 1967 and 1968. More than 50,000 Americans arrived at the Mall in Washington on October 21, 1967, to protest U.S. involvement in Vietnam. In January 1968, a six-month battle for Khe Sanh began, which was followed by the communist forces' Tet Offensive. North Vietnamese troops launched a major surprise attack against U.S. and South Vietnamese forces as the lunar New Year celebrations began. During the incursion, the North Vietnamese seized province capitals throughout South Vietnam, and brazenly invaded the U.S. Embassy in Saigon. While the North Vietnamese forces paid a heavy toll in lost lives, the bold maneuver turned the tide of the war for Vietnam and became a media nightmare for President Johnson. Many experts speculate that this raid was the final nail in the coffin of the president's 1968 re-election bid.

Johnson's decision not to run opened the door for the election of President Richard Nixon in November 1968. One of the new president's first major decisions on Vietnam was to escalate the conflict by launching a major air strike against Cambodia the following March. He pledged to end the war in six months, and announced the withdrawal of 25,000 U.S. troops from Saigon on June 8, 1969. But the war didn't end and protests at home continued with increasing ferocity. This time around, more than 250,000 people rallied on The Mall in November 1969. Unfortunately for the protestors, the war machine kept growing as the first draft since World War II was announced the following month, countering the president's promise to end the war and bring the troops home.

Introduction of the draft set off near-revolt as young people organized against the war on campuses across the country. Teach-ins, student-led rallies and marches took place across the nation, leading to a deep chasm between generations and between classes of Americans. The anti-war movement was widespread and unlike anything seen before in American history.

The cause had a powerful musical and Hollywood influence that fueled its attention and provided a common language and style for protesters across the nation. The resulting speeches, music and literature reflected a deep anger and hopelessness over the Vietnam War that was felt by significant numbers of Americans. The protest culture was so powerful that soldiers overseas even began supporting the movement in a variety of ways, including stitching peace symbols on their uniforms and refusing direct orders.

And in a complete reversal of respect and adulation shown toward soldiers returning from World War II, protesters subjected American soldiers coming home from Vietnam to taunts of "baby killers" and other disparaging names. The soldiers were regularly verbally and physically abused on the streets of America's small towns and big cities alike. This was a far cry from the hero's welcome received by previous American military forces.

The war continued to escalate as Cambodia was invaded by U.S. and South Vietnamese troops in 1970 in an effort to oust North Vietnamese troops. The invasion only increased the protests, speeches, rallies and riots at home. Campuses across the country were in flames, and the resulting protests led to one of the worst moments in American history and the deaths of students at Kent State University. The student deaths would come to symbolize the depth of division, fear and chaos that existed between government and its citizens during the Vietnam era. Trust in government would be forever changed a little after noon on May 4.

A full-weekend schedule of anti-war protests began on campus shortly after the formal announcement of the U.S. invasion of Cambodia. The student protests grew from campus-centered events, to activities throughout downtown Kent, Ohio. Students ravaged the town, causing widespread property damage and setting off a wave of fear among local residents. The student activity prompted Kent's mayor to call on the governor and National Guard for assistance, which arrived Saturday evening.

Chaos reigned as the National Guardsmen tried to restore order. Students and townspeople were divided, their reactions to Cambodia mixed. Some students participated in clean-up efforts while others bombed the Army R.O.T.C. headquarters on campus.

The governor held a press conference Sunday afternoon, calling for calm and informing citizens that the university would remain open in spite of the weekend's chaotic activity. Calm did settle in — for the day.

A student-planned anti-war rally began the next day, and was expected to draw between 2,000 and 3,000 people to the center of campus. The National Guard tried dispersing the gathering, which spurred some protesters to shower them with verbal assaults and rocks. In response, the Guard volleyed tear gas, which was rendered useless by the gusty spring winds, into the crowd. Guardsmen pushed on, trying to enforce the Ohio Riot Act. In an effort to prove their determination and seriousness, soldiers affixed bayonets to their weapons and pushed the protesters back.

Events spiraled out of control and a peaceful rally turned deadly as soldiers wheeled and fired upon protesters in front of the Taylor Hall parking lot. Four students were killed, and another nine were wounded by the nearly 70 rounds fired by the Guardsmen. The governor and university officials closed the school later that day in response to the tragedy. But the wounds inflicted that weekend persisted in the community and many of the scars remain today.

American involvement in Vietnam continued, as did the protester disruptions at home. The turmoil continued for several years as the death toll rose in Vietnam and student-led protests at home grew in frequency and ferocity. The resulting civil unrest put pressure on the American government to pull out of Vietnam, which it agreed to do after signing the Paris Peace Accords on January 23, 1973. Signing of the treaty meant that South Vietnam would have to fight the North on its own moving forward.

The South Vietnamese ultimately lost that battle when North Vietnamese troops took control of Saigon, on April 30, 1975, leading to the nation's surrender.

Outcomes

The war in Vietnam ended for America in the mid-1970s, but the damage inflicted upon our nation, specifically in terms of trust in government and its leaders, was significant and far-reaching. As stated earlier, trust in government fell by more than 20 percent in the years immediately following Vietnam. In that short time, the number of Americans who trusted government to do the right thing dropped to slightly more than 50 percent!

America's new-found cynicism reared its ugly head at the ballot box as well. Nearly 61 percent of eligible Americans voted in 1968. Participation dropped precipitously in 1972, as Vietnam's battles and protests reached a fever pitch. Only 55 percent of eligible Americans voted. This trend continued throughout the seventies as new events continued to erode American trust in government and its leaders.

It is staggering to think that in a mere decade, America could move from a prosperous, optimistic and trusting nation, to one where more than half of its citizens distrusted their leaders and were fearful of the future.

Chapter 7

Watergate and the Nixon Years: The Roots of Apathy and Cynicism

Americans were reeling in the late 1960s and early 1970s from the casualties of war and cultural division. President Nixon came to power in November of 1968, after beating Hubert Humphrey by 510,000 votes. President Nixon certainly didn't have a mandate from the American people, earning a mere 43 percent of the popular vote.

As outlined in the previous section, President Nixon's administration inherited numerous obstacles related to Vietnam. However, his ultimate downfall was self-inflicted. Nixon's infamous Watergate scandal culminated in resignation — the first in American history — and the cementing of American distrust of elected officials.

The Watergate scandal grew from a plot hatched and carried out by President Nixon and key leaders within his administration. Public confidence in Nixon's plans to end the war in Vietnam crumbled, leading to increased pressure and scrutiny of Administration policies on both the domestic and international fronts. The president became convinced that a coordinated attack was being led by anti-war activists to undermine his administration, which limited his chances for re-election in 1972.

And so, on June 17, 1971, the president endorsed a plan created by Tom Charles Huston to conduct covert espionage activities that included burglaries, surveillance, training of campus informants and a host of other illegal actions. All of these techniques were intended to neutralize the president's political opposition. President Nixon likened his counterattack on anti-war forces to the McCarthy witch-hunt — a campaign that justified slander, character assassination and political tricks against any viable enemy.

Nixon led an intentional, full-scale assault that utilized any available weapon to destroy his challengers. The plan was implemented as the U.S. economy lost steam and declined. This increased pressure on the administration as they saw and felt a significant erosion of the nation's trust in their president and approval of his job performance.

On June 17, 1972, Washington, D.C., police arrested five men who had broken into the Democratic National Committee headquarters in the Watergate Hotel. The group, under the direction of G. Gordon Liddy and E. Howard Hunt, were attempting to repair a surveillance bug that had been placed during a previous secret entry into the office. The break-in and surveillance were part of the larger espionage plan authorized by President Nixon.

In an effort to explain the activity, the apprehended criminals stated the covert actions were part of a national security investigation to see if Howard Hughes — a businessman allegedly intertwined with the CIA and espionage — had provided money to the Democratic Party. President Nixon distanced himself from the activity by claiming it was a "third-rate burglary."

The President's approval ratings hovered between 60 percent to 66 percent from the time of the Watergate break-in to the conviction of those involved in the illegal activity. Yet citizen support for the president evaporated as information surfaced that directly implicated him in the break-in plot and subsequent cover-up. Perhaps most damaging to the president's credibility was the revelation from his chief counsel, John Dean, that Nixon approved on June 23, 1972, the use of money to quiet his Watergate burglars. Dean went so far as to say that the president not only signed-off on the activity, but that he knew where money could be found to ensure the burglars' silence.

The plot grew increasingly insidious as Attorney General John Mitchell agreed to "acquire" $220,000 for the hush fund if his friend Henry Tasca was appointed ambassador to Greece. About the same time, it became apparent to the American public that President Nixon encouraged the phony cover-up story told to the FBI. As reported to the public, the president said that deep-cover CIA assets were involved in the break-in. And the FBI was warned not to dig too deeply. This direct intervention by President Nixon resulted in obstruction of justice charges that would ultimately force him from office.

At this point, the president's approval ratings plummeted to roughly 30 percent, which was one of the lowest in history at that time — only to be matched by President George W. Bush's in 2005. All along, President Nixon stated publicly that he had no knowledge of, or involvement in, the break-in or cover-up. He even went so far as to call for intensive inquiries into who was behind the crimes. These lies ultimately deepened the nation's distrust when the truth finally came out.

President Nixon's troubles grew when reports surfaced that secret Oval Office tapes existed that held the truth about Watergate and its cover-up. Sen. Sam Ervin, chair of the Senate Watergate Committee and Special Prosecutor Archibald Cox sought to recover the tapes, and then took their request to the Supreme Court after Nixon refused to cooperate. The president lost the battle eight to zero and was forced to turn the tapes over because, as the court stated, executive privilege didn't apply in this case. Because of the pressure from Cox and others, President Nixon ordered the Special Prosecutor fired on October 20, 1973. These events are known as the Saturday Night Massacre because numerous staff members and appointees either quit in protest or were fired. The president first asked Attorney General Elliott Richardson to fire Cox. Richardson refused and resigned. Next, Deputy Attorney General William Ruckelshaus also refused Nixon's order to fire Cox, and he resigned in protest. Finally, Assistant Attorney General Robert Bork agreed to fire Cox and executed the president's order. Americans were enraged by this activity, and the president's approval ratings dropped below 30 percent.

The Saturday Night Massacre also prompted an unprecedented action by *Time Magazine*. The publication wrote its first editorial in history, which called for the president's resignation. Finally, the U.S. House of Representatives debated the matter and passed articles of impeachment that charged President Nixon with failure to execute the law as required, obstruction of justice, abuse of power and sabotaging the American democratic process. Evidence disclosed in the House led members of the president's own party to warn him that a conviction would pass the Senate unless he agreed to resign.

And so, President Nixon resigned on August 8, 1974 with an approval rating slightly higher than 20 percent — the lowest of any president in American history. Reporters and journalists took care throughout the crisis to report only what was corroborated by sources. And as a result, the American people thoroughly trusted the negative news they were reading and watching.

But it wasn't just the president's actions surrounding Watergate that damaged government's credibility at that time. Prior to Watergate, Nixon's second in command, Vice President Spiro Agnew resigned amid accusations of income tax evasion, bribery, conspiracy and extortion. Initially, Agnew vigorously proclaimed his innocence to the American people. But in the end, he was convicted of the charges, fined $10,000 and placed on three year's probation. This situation only reinforced the growing perception among Americans that their leaders were corrupt and would do anything to secure political power and personal gain.

Vice President Gerald Ford, who replaced Agnew, ascended to the presidency after Nixon resigned. In an unprecedented maneuver, the new president pardoned Richard Nixon in September of 1974, deepening the nation's cynicism and distrust of government. President Ford apparently agonized over the decision and felt it was the best way to close the chapter on the previous administration, allowing the nation to focus on the future instead of the past. In his national address announcing the pardon, President Ford claimed that, "the long national nightmare is over."

In 1974, only 36 percent of Americans trusted government to do the right thing. And in 1976, voter turnout dropped again, to just below 60 percent of registered voters. Unfortunately, President Ford was wrong. In terms of cynicism and apathy, the long national nightmare had just begun.

Chapter 8

The Fourth Estate: Media Spur American Political Cynicism and Apathy

Media coverage of Vietnam and Watergate added to the events' negative legacy. During Vietnam, an expanding television empire brought the carnage and chaos home for viewers through daily death counts and "facts" that didn't necessarily jive with the eventual outcomes. Foreign coverage of Vietnam, suddenly available to Americans via PBS, presented an interminably grim picture of the war, one far different than the more neutral view painted by American elected officials and reported by Mainstream American Media outlets.

Watergate also unfolded due to a particularly active media, with reporters like Woodward and Bernstein of the *Washington Post* breaking news of the scandal through secret informants such as the infamous "Deep Throat," whose identity wasn't disclosed until recently.

Members of the media began to evolve from reporters of the news to commentators, often adding opinions to the story. This was particularly true as television became a 24-hour, seven-day-a-week beast that needed constant "feeding" to survive. As a result, news cycles contained details that in some cases simultaneously titillated and yet turned viewers off. Future sections of this book will examine the cycle of neglect operating between elected officials and the voting public. But for now, it is sufficient to understand that today's media attempt to fill the void that exists between politicians and citizens who are not communicating directly about issues that matter to communities across the nation. And in the process, media bias, "framing" and punditry actually further divide politicians and voters, instead of facilitating a better and more frequent dialogue.

Since Vietnam and Watergate, the media have placed a negative filter (perhaps understandably) over their reporting, frequently presenting elections and candidate coverage as a game, not as a substantive examination of issues and platforms. James Fallows, a scholar on media and politics, compares today's modern coverage of elections to sports analysis. And other scholars like Thomas Patterson believe that reporters are too close to elections, scandal and ongoing policy debates to cover them objectively. As a result, their stories are clouded by a "waterfront cynicism."

Patterson believes that political reporters have spent too much time reporting from the West Wing, the campaign bus, the Pentagon, etc., and not enough time discussing issues with average citizens. So their stories tend to be written more for other reporters, and less for the people reading or watching their coverage. Patterson, Fallows and other scholars on the subject share one basic message: Today's media do not simply report the news. Instead, they are commentators who interpret the news for their audiences, coloring and shaping it based upon their own beliefs, cynicisms and perspective. This is especially true of tired campaign reporters who have heard candidates give the same stump speeches over and over, or the media following legislative battles in Congress day after day.

Some scholars, Fallows in particular, believe campaign coverage has become a "horse race." The amount of money a candidate has raised, his or her likelihood of victory and other factors become the most important elements of news coverage. This happens at the expense of examining issues or policies offered by candidates, which would help the viewer or reader make his/her own substantively informed decision. Campaign coverage, then, is less about the policies recommended by a candidate and more about how they are polling with specific "swing voters" or how well their message played with media-convened focus groups.

In short, reporters are sharing less substantive information about candidates, reducing elections to battles of style, character and fundraising prowess. Just listen the next time a reporter on your TV set is discussing an ongoing campaign. Do they say candidate x, "offered four proposals for ending the Iraq War and bringing our troops home?" Or do they say candidate x "offered his same four proposals today on the Iraq War that are intended to woo swing voters in Iowa?" Through the latter statement, reporters are framing the news for their audience, oftentimes implying that a candidate is simply pandering to potential voters in a specific area or of a certain ideology.

This kind of coverage erodes positive perceptions by citizens and instead implies that candidates and elected officials are simply doing and saying whatever is necessary to win. This mediated framing of candidate positions compromises viewers' opinions. They are less open to the possibility that a candidate may be offering proposals based on deeply-held convictions, powerful personal experiences or extensive research. And instead suggests they are making decisions based on a singular desire to leap ahead in the latest poll.

This type of coverage makes tuning out the news and politics guilt-free for Americans. After all, why should someone remain engaged if campaign news coverage doesn't appear to be based on actual facts, and is instead, just another medium for candidates to sling mud at one another and pander to the public?

Reflecting on history, it is clear that Americans weren't always this way. As outlined in previous chapters, a large majority of citizens trusted elected officials and candidates prior to Vietnam. And they went to the polls in larger numbers. The Vietnam War, Watergate and numerous other scandals sewed the seeds of the cynicism and apathy that took root in the mid-1960s. Media added fertilizer to the seeds of distrust and disinterest, portraying events in a manner that frames candidates and government leaders merely swinging with the tide of polls, focus groups and public opinion.

Since their inception, media have been a powerful tool for influencing public opinion and they have undoubtedly changed public perception of politics and campaigns. Americans formerly viewed politics as a powerful if somewhat esoteric entity that impacted their daily lives. Now, they see parties as an out-of-control machine fueled by obsessions with image, victory and personal profit. By covering every twist and turn of a campaign so exhaustively, media coverage in effect makes politics seem boring and irrelevant.

Ironically, it appears that the very framing and bias that pervades coverage has also made the media objects of distrust or at least suspicion. Viewers now take their candidates and their news with a grain of salt. According to a 2004 Reuters/DecisionQuest study, newspaper and television reporters received a "C" for trustworthiness. And TV reporters are trusted less today than they were a few short years ago. Only 43 percent of viewers believe what they see as compared to 39 percent of newspaper readers.

Future sections of this book will outline ways to combat cynicism and disengagement. But it's important to point out that hope does exist even though this section portrayed a negative perception of current American politics and the media. Kate Santich, a reporter for the *Orlando Sentinel* compared cynics to a warm grilled cheese sandwich.

"They are crunchy on the outside, soft and gooey on the inside. They are idealists in drag." Americans want to believe that a storybook life is possible. They believe they can be rich, famous, possess all the spoils of capitalism and ride off into the sunset. Think about it — Hollywood, *People Magazine* and countless other purveyors of the "American Dream" would be obsolete if this weren't the case.

That's why it is critical for elected officials to get beyond the lens of media framing. They must engage citizens, working on issues and solutions together and inspiring them to action. People respond and participate when they know they are welcomed into the political process.

Americans from all walks of life have a stake in government decision-making. Legislation happens. It's just a question of whether it happens with citizens or to them. And that's why they must take a step to engage their leaders as well.

Election Day doesn't end a voter's responsibility. They must also engage their newly-elected officials — whether they voted for them or not — to ensure that their needs are being met and their voices heard. It is not too utopian an idea to think that politicians and citizens working closely together will force the media to become reporters again, instead of pundits. By breaking the voter/politician cycle of neglect, the 24-hour media beast would be forced to provide more substance, less sizzle. And voters would have more information on which to base their vote and more ammunition for getting legislation passed that behooves their community.

Baby Boomers started the disengagement trend during Vietnam and Watergate, but their children are mastering it. Future sections of this book will focus on the missed opportunities for engaging young people in the political process. In the end, cynicism and apathy are serious barriers to participation and must be reversed if we are to end the decades-long trend of growing distrust in the American political system.

Section III

Chapters 9 — 13

Barriers to Active Citizenship: The Civic Tri-axiom.

Chapter 9

Introduction: The Cycle of Neglect

The facts, stories and case studies detailed throughout this book will articulate a pervasive attitude of uncertainty, distrust and disregard for government among a significant portion of Americans. This is evident in their attitudes toward government's accomplishments (or in some cases, lack thereof) and their daily activities, which tend to lie outside the civic realm. The evidence also comes from a broad citizen unwillingness to engage in the civic process.

Many reasons exist to explain away or rationalize this persistent attitude. A number of these reasons were articulated in previous chapters — war, scandal and government *over*promising and *under*delivering on results. In this section of the book, we'll examine a more concrete explanation for citizen disengagement — a theory known as the Civic Triaxiom. Before delving into the theory we must examine an overarching theme tied into the civic triaxiom that limits desire for involvement — "The Cycle of Neglect."

Participation in America's representative form of government requires active engagement and dialogue between citizens and the people we elect to represent us. When this system breaks down, individuals lose a voice in the halls of government and power over the legislation, ordinances and regulations that make up America's "rule of law." Currently, the interplay between citizens and government officials is not working effectively, and many people are feeling disenfranchised and discouraged as a result. A cycle of neglect exists in which elected officials do not reach out to average citizens because they do not vote, send letters, phone calls or e-mails of concern over issues, and they do not contribute financially to campaigns. And, as a result, many citizens feel government is unresponsive and holds minimal connection to their daily lives. Taking a closer look at this phenomenon will provide a clearer picture of how we arrived at this point in the civic process.

As outlined in the previous section of this book, overall civic participation has been on the decline since the early 1970s. More relevant to the discussion of the cycle of neglect, voter participation has declined significantly. Elected officials look around the electoral landscape and see increasing numbers of citizens sitting on the sidelines, unwilling to participate. Legislators need help understanding the impact their votes will have on the economy, the environment, our health care system and a range of other issues that affect citizens on local, state and national levels.

Unfortunately, the heavy legislative calendar doesn't allow time for elected officials to truly gain a detailed perspective on all sides of the issues involved in a given legislative proposal. Furthermore, these officials are average citizens, just like you and me. And they don't always know the fine points of every issue that comes across their desk. It's simply not possible, and it wasn't the intention of our Founding Fathers, who foresaw a system where citizens actively discussed the issues with their elected representatives. And that's why elected officials need assistance when casting votes for pending legislation.

In Washington, D.C., in the many legislative offices around the capital, there is an army of "Hill staffers" working to ensure the tough choices are made with as much thought and foresight as possible. But these resources just don't exist for most elected officials at the state and local levels of government. Exactly 41 of America's 50 state governments work on a "part-time" basis, meaning they do not operate year-round. For a host of obvious reasons, this leads to a less robust staff structure at the state level than the one in Washington. And local governments (counties, cities, towns, villages, etc.) have even fewer resources.

In fact, many state legislators rely on a staff of one or two people to do everything from constituent services (answering requests ranging from assistance with state scholarship issues or tax questions to voter registration challenges) to providing answers to complex legislation. In some cases, state legislative offices consist of an administrative assistant, who, among myriad other things, is responsible for answering phones, keeping the elected official's schedule, making copies of legislation, hearing requests, etc.; and a legislative aide, who is more often than not, a college intern. And so, they need our help.

Oftentimes, they turn to lobbyists — individuals or special interest groups advocating issues of importance to their constituents or clients. For the most part, lobbyists are decent and honest people who use facts and statistics to show why an elected official should vote for or against pending legislation. But as common sense suggests, the less voters and average citizens engage in this process, the more elected officials rely on lobbyists and other, perhaps more biased "voices." These include newspapers, radio talk show hosts, political action committees (PACs), etc. And that's exactly what is happening as fewer and fewer people contact their elected officials about issues that matter to them or vote for the officials they think will best represent their concerns.

Elected officials, under the pressure of a tight legislative calendar, stop reaching out to significant portions of our population, who through their inaction, have made it clear they don't want to participate in the legislative process. Elected officials don't have the time to chase disengaged voters; therefore, they stop looking to them for answers. And on a number of levels, this is completely understandable.

In turn, a significant segment of American citizens believe most elected officials do not care, or at least focus, on their needs or issues. And as a result, they tune out or turn to other forms of civic expression, like volunteerism as a catalyst for changing the world around them. According to a recent poll, nearly three-quarters of Americans believe that elected officials lose touch with their voters' needs and ideals when they arrive in Washington. This number is slightly lower than in the early 1990s, when distrust of government and elected officials was running at a premium due to the political scandals and significant upheaval in Congressional politics that were outlined previously.

Furthermore, only about 39 percent of surveyed Americans believe elected officials care about voter opinions. This is particularly true among young people who see elected officials tackling legislation related to Medicare, Social Security and other issues benefiting senior citizens, and feel their voice is lost. They'd prefer that elected officials focus on education, crime and the environment. But what these young people fail to realize is that approximately 80 percent of 80-year-olds vote, and 20 percent of 20-year-olds vote. This statistical gap accounts for the types of issues being discussed in government at all levels. In the end, this becomes a self-fulfilling prophecy as those turning away from the system reinforce the cycle of neglect.

A point briefly mentioned above needs closer examination because it points to the challenge of only volunteering and not closing the loop by engaging in the civic process. As stated previously, many people have decided to forgo direct political engagement to pursue voleerism. But by turning only to volunteerism, these citizens are failing to get at the root causes of the issues that matter most to them. Volunteerism is important. But done in a vacuum, it doesn't solve the problems facing our society. Mentoring, literacy programs, cleaning parks and building homes for low-income people are important measures of how Americans care for each other and struggle to pick up the things that slip through the cracks of legislative remedy.

Yet, these issues and problems — no matter how passionately they're tackled and no matter how much human capital we invest — will not be solved purely by citizen service. These issues must be attacked at their root cause, which often requires government action and citizen involvement in the legislative process.

Literacy programs slowly, incrementally, impact the segment of the American population that can't read. One-by-one, volunteers teach people the basics of reading and writing to help provide the skills that will improve their quality of life. But wouldn't it be more efficient, and ultimately more effective, to engage in the legislative process to tackle this issue at its roots? Shouldn't these volunteers also be looking at the larger explanations for the problems they're working so passionately to solve? In the end then, shouldn't these volunteers be advocating for increased teacher accountability, local control and compensation? Shouldn't they be working proactively to identify funding or testing mechanisms that will improve our schools? The obvious answer is yes. The laudable civic service must be matched by an equally active interaction with government.

For the most part, engaging in the legislative process allows us to impact the most people in the shortest amount of time. The same is true for environmental issues. Monitoring our waterways, cleaning local parks or highways and other efforts to maintain our environment have gone a long way towards improving the quality of life in communities around this nation. Yet focusing solely on volunteer service activities will not improve regulations for construction site practices, factory discharges in waterways or a host of other legislative and regulatory remedies that could significantly improve our environment. Greater protections and "repairs" can be accomplished by working with government, instead of turning a back to the legislative process.

We'll examine some successful case studies for turning passion into action later in this book. Ultimately, we can boil the cycle of neglect down to one statement: Legislation happens. It's just a question of whether it happens with you, or to you. And in this case, many Americans are letting legislation happen to them.

Chapter 10

The Civic Tri-Axiom — Institutional Access

While there are many causes for our diminishing levels of civic participation, three major categorical obstacles limit activity in the United States. The three barriers, or Civic Tri-axiom, include "institutional access," a "loss of civic responsibility" and "life factors." In this chapter, we'll examine institutional access — a busy society curbs individual involvement because myriad institutional road blocks, including: one-day polling at a specific location for registered voters, long lines at the Department of Motor Vehicles, lack of response to citizen contact with elected officials, and an array of other challenges.

Barriers to Voting

Several factors inherent in the operation of state and federal government (and some laws) prohibit widespread, active participation in the electoral process. These regulations prevent easy access to the polls for an increasingly diverse and busy society. With the exception of absentee voting and a few state statutes, government laws combine to limit citizen voting to one day, at designated polling places, during fixed polling hours.

The most notable exception to this rule, which would go a long way towards improving participation if enhanced, is absentee voting. The current voting system presents an increasing number of challenges for average citizens as they have to take time away from demanding work schedules, fight traffic, get children to and from daycare, or other life factors they may face in our increasingly harried modern society. This requires a greater level of commitment from voters to actually participate.

And as will become clear in the next chapter, citizens are not being taught the basic skills of active participation, which spurs the desire to be involved, regardless of what roadblocks may pop up. As a result, the electoral process takes a back seat to pressing personal issues as Americans put more and more activities on their plates.

Making Government Work *for All People*

Voting is not the only aspect of civic participation that is impacted by institutional roadblocks. As a free market society, we've come to expect high quality, timely service and competitive prices from the many vendors and service providers we encounter on a daily basis. People get frustrated by long wait times when calling to dispute a phone or electric bill. Consumers stop shopping at places that don't have a variety of products to choose from or offer fair prices. As free market consumers, we've come to expect these vendors to meet our needs on our terms.

But when it comes to government services, America's legions of Amazon.com, e-Bay consumers do not choose to engage. Most Americans interact with government because we have to, not out of choice or an appreciation for high-quality service. So the ultimate challenge for government lies in converting these passive consumers of public services into responsible, supportive citizens who make their voices heard because they understand the necessity and responsibility of participation. Most levels of government, while huge in scope and cost, do little to actively engage Americans in a meaningful way. The old models of government — offices that provide services, send out checks, and "help" with problems — simply aren't meeting the needs of the 21st century American. So we must look to successful models that work for and with people. And for that, we must look to the private sector. Consider a few key principles for effective delivery of service that government can borrow from the business world:

- **Customer service is key!** Organizations that provide it win business and keep customers. Those that don't, lose them. The same applies to government. Citizens will be more inclined to participate if government can slash long waiting lines, put more services on the Internet, change the digital divide into digital opportunity and make sure constituent calls don't reach a busy signal. This also means government needs to reduce the number of "executives" working in middle management, while providing more customer service representatives empowered to make decisions and facilitate requests by telephone and online.
- **Use TV, radio, and the Internet to inform and mobilize citizens.** Counties, cities and even some states are discovering that interactive government services — including TV and the Internet — help foster connections between citizens and government. A "connected" person is more likely to pursue good government,

to participate in decision-making and to vote. Radio ad spots reinforce government messages about available services and how to access them. Web sites and TV programming provide detailed information about legislation, public forums and other government activities.

- **Promises made, promises kept.** A key to success for government, just like business, is fulfilling promises. When government lives up to its guarantee of effective constituent service, citizens are more likely to overcome their apathy and engage in their community. Basic things like receiving accurate and speedy answers to questions, being transferred to the right department the first time or hearing a friendly voice on the other end of the phone can help people feel government is working for them. And they will be more likely to reach out for information or participate following a good experience.

- **The C-SPAN effect** — government magnified for real people. By taking public cameras into Congress, the courts, and into American communities, C-SPAN has revolutionized the way Americans are able to view their government in action and in context. By expanding this concept to showcase government agencies and service-providers in action, increasing the number of non-cable channels offering such coverage, and creating interactive Internet sites to ensure "follow-through" for people, government can and will begin to make more sense to Americans — creating a government truly "of the people, by the people and for the people."

The federal government and agencies at various state and local levels across America are realizing the need to function like 21st century consumers have come to expect from businesses they deal with each day. Many are taking steps to update their services and systems. These efforts have achieved various levels of success. One positive example comes from a few states that began transforming labor offices (often referred to as "unemployment offices/lines") into education facilities that harness the power of the Internet and online learning to improve employee skills while posting job listings in real-time. People will come to government when they see it as an effective and indispensable tool of success.

Improving Voter Turnout Through Motor Voter

The National Voter Registration Act of 1993, which made voting easier, is another example of government responding to the needs of its citizens. The law, also known as the "Motor Voter Bill," was signed in time for the 1994 election and:

- Established procedures that increase the number of voters eligible for federal elections.
- Protected the integrity of the electoral process by ensuring that voter registration rolls are more accurately created and maintained.
- Encouraged more eligible citizens to cast votes in federal elections. It achieves these results by:

  — Giving eligible citizens a greater number of locations and opportunities to register to vote.
  — Requiring the appropriate agencies to follow more-stringent, uniform and non-discriminatory policies and procedures for accurately identifying and removing ineligible voters from the rolls.

— Detailing fail-safe voting procedures that ensure that an individual's right to participate prevails over current bureaucratic or legal technicalities.

Finally, Motor Voter allows citizens the opportunity to register to vote when they obtain a driver's license, which is where the law gets its name. The issuing state agency is required to ask license recipients if they are registered to vote or if they need to update voter information at the time of license renewal. Drivers can update their home address or register, right then and there, with minimal additional effort.

Motor Voter has received moderately passing marks to date. The system has improved voting rights protections, removed thousands of ineligible voters from the rolls and clarified a broad system of registration and eligibility requirements faced by state and local government bureaucrats. However, it has not increased the overall registration and voter participation of eligible citizens.

Roughly 70 percent of America's Voting Aged Population (VAP) was registered to vote in 2002, a decline from 71.55 percent in 1998. Motor Voter advocates and some government officials contend this dip in registration is due to Motor Voter's effectiveness at removing ineligible voters from the rolls. But this argument doesn't hold water. America has a larger pool of eligible voters today, so in the end, the law hasn't elevated the number of people registered as hoped for by the original empowering legislation.

In order for government to effectively bring its operations into the 21st century, leaders must begin a dialogue with citizens about needs and expectations. Fortunately, some state governments have created task forces to study changes that would make voter services more reliable, accountable and timely.

Government Response to Election 2000

Changes to the voting system in the wake of Election 2000 are a prime example of government seeking citizen input to overhaul and modernize its operations. The 2000 Presidential Election was one of the closest and most hotly contested of all time. And the outcome was in dispute in large part because of the government's reliance on malfunctioning, or at the least outdated, election systems and other institutional barriers to participation.

According to a study and computer analysis of the election by the Caltech/MIT Voting Technology Project, the ballots of between four to six million voters were not accurately counted. Nearly 1.5 million of those voters actually cast ballots for president, but their voices weren't heard due to the infamous hanging or pregnant chads, misaligned ballots or other errors with the voting system. Another one to three million Americans didn't even make it to the ballot box because they were inaccurately purged from the voter rolls or didn't appear on lists at their voting precinct. And according to the study, another 500,000 to more than one million Americans didn't vote because of other electoral system malfunctions or prohibitively long waits at the polling precinct.

The same Caltech/MIT study claims errors were even more prevalent on "down-ballot races" (elections further down the list, like U.S. Senators, governors, etc.). State and local elections are usually decided by narrow margins. The study predicted that many of the outcomes could be overturned or altered if the system worked more effectively and had accurately counted voter intentions.

Unfortunately, malfunctioning voter machines aren't the only barriers to active electoral participation. Too often, voters do not know their rights and are turned away from the polls for a host of reasons. According to just about every study of the electoral process, countless voters are turned away from the polls because they don't know their fundamental rights, or poll workers fail to accurately enforce the law.

To combat this problem, state and local governments should develop and post voter rights at each precinct. Some of the basic information these postings should contain, include:

- Voters are allowed to cast a ballot if they are already in line when the polls close
- Voters can ask for a new ballot if they make a mistake or want to alter their vote
- Voters are allowed to ask for and receive assistance from poll workers
- Voters are allowed to cast provisional ballots — a citizen can vote even if a discrepancy exists over his or her eligibility. They are allowed to cast a ballot, which is then sealed and set aside for later consideration, once their eligibility is verified. It is counted if the voter is accurately registered and discarded if he or she is not.

Another barrier, in line with the discussion of pulling government into the 21st century, is the use of obsolete voting technology. Many studies contend that the 2000 election would not have been so close had different, more effective voting systems been used around the nation. Nearly 32 percent of Americans used some form of punch card machine, which utilizes a stylus to "break" a chad of paper on a ballot. This is the system voters used in the contested Florida precincts.

Nearly 16 percent of voters cast ballots on mechanical machines. This system is so outdated that rumors exist claiming some coastal states sought to purchase them for use as the building blocks of coral reef communities in American waterways. In other words, these machines are old, break down and are good only for rusting in a manner conducive to giving coral a place to call home. Not exactly the system we want utilized to decide important elections! An additional 29 percent of voters in 2000 used optical-scan technology (filling in a circle or box with a number two pencil, just like in high school), 12 percent used direct recording electric machines ("touch screen" systems), another 0.5 percent still used paper ballots and the remaining 10 percent lived in counties that utilize a combination of systems.

In the time shortly after the election, only a handful of states had taken significant strides to overhaul their voting systems in order to avoid becoming the butt of jokes like Florida in 2000. Many of the initial states like Florida, Georgia and Maryland, who utilized citizen and expert input to modernize their systems, are undergoing intense scrutiny. In Georgia for instance, elected officials are now calling for printable "receipts" to be incorporated into the electoral system. The hope is that fraud can be prevented and a level of trust instilled in citizens that their vote was counted accurately. In the end, these efforts have had moderate success in making voting easier and more accurate.

Their reforms also included the strengthening of voter rights, a mandate to use the most modern voting technology and improvements to the poll worker education system. Georgia's reforms went the furthest and took place in the shortest amount of time. Secretary of State Cathy Cox recruited election experts, business leaders, elected officials, community leaders and other citizens to serve on a task force charged with improving the election process to prevent future electoral snafus.

The resulting 21st Century Voting Commission produced a report that led to significant alterations of Georgia's voting system. These included the creation of a statewide electronic voting system — the first of its kind in America — that placed "touch screen" voting machines in every precinct around the state within one year. As outlined above, these actions are under political and legal scrutiny. And in the case of Secretary Cox, these actions are credited in part with dooming her 2006 Democratic Primary bid for governor.

The federal government finally took action on the election system reform front in 2002 when it passed legislation that provided funds and "guidance" for states and local governments seeking to modernize their systems. The resulting Help America Vote Act (HAVA) provided federal funds to states for elections if they complied with a list of guidelines and requirements. These included:

- Mandating voting system and polling place accessibility for people with disabilities
- Creation and management of a statewide electronic voter database
- New requirements for voter registration
- A mandate for provisional balloting
- Better education about the electoral process and voter rights (with prominent visibility of those rights at polling places)

A number of states took less comprehensive action to reform their systems immediately following HAVA's passage. By 2003, nearly 45 states had considered HAVA-related bills. But only 36 states ended up passing the legislation, and only 24 of those passed laws that were relatively comprehensive in their compliance with HAVA.

Conclusion

The lessons here are a bit murky. Through cooperation and dialogue, government can take steps to remove some of the immediate institutional challenges to active citizen participation. Some will argue that government isn't going far enough. And as evidenced throughout this section, it looks like many public sector leaders are beginning to realize that government must become more effective and accessible if it is to invite citizen participation. And as a result, the pace of government reform is likely to increase in the years to come.

This chapter provided just a few examples of government working to remedy the institutional access problem facing citizens, which adds to their disinterest in participating in the civic process. Case studies exist in every corner of the nation, and at every level of government. Some programs have been innovative and successful, while others have not. What is also becoming clear through the modernization process is that it's not just government's role to fix this problem. Citizens also have a responsibility for active participation, no matter how significant the barriers. And finally, education — particularly civic education — is a central element of this undertaking and key to increasing public demand for access changes. We'll examine this theme thoroughly in the next chapter.

Chapter 11

The Civic Tri-Axiom: Missing Fundamentals of Civic Participation

It is imperative to teach our newest citizens the core values of civic responsibility. Like any other life skill, voting is a habit that must be taught at an early age in order to be effective. As a result, we must begin teaching students these important lessons in the earliest levels of our school systems if we intend to make a long-term impact on the problem of voter apathy and nonparticipation.

Many nonprofit and community organizations across the country share this mission and offer programming for America's youth in the hopes of salvaging democracy as we know it. Organizations like Kids Vote USA are working with schools around the country to introduce or expand civic education in the classroom. The problem is that little state and local institutional support exists, and the programs are incredibly costly due to teacher training, printing and copying of materials, and the development of other program elements for all students.

Local governments and school boards across the country already have some form of civic education in their curriculums, but most are not taught throughout the year or from K through 12th grade. Nevertheless, these efforts are a critical first step in minimizing the number of citizens that hold a negative view of government or choose not to be involved in the civic process.

Numerous studies on voting behavior point to the necessity and recent successes of civic education. Studies completed at Stanford University conclude that voter turnout increased in Kids Vote USA communities by five to 10 percent each election. Stanford University analysts credited Kids Vote's education and information sharing activities with the increased turnout.

But it's not just our young people that many of these programs hope to impact. Many civic education efforts like Kids Vote seek to teach parents of students receiving the information through classroom activities and projects. Through these projects, information on the electoral process, candidate biographies and key election year issues are transmitted to children who take it home to their parents.

A central component of the Kids Vote program is mock elections, which are held for children in concert with real election cycles. The mock elections energize children, who in turn, encourage their parents to take them to the polls. And in the end, the experience leaves an indelible mark on the minds of children about the excitement and importance of voting.

The role of these school programs in increasing voter turnout and energizing and educating the electorate can't be underestimated. According to the Stanford researchers, a welcomed side effect is the "ability of lower income Kids Vote students to motivate non-voting parents into second political socialization," or what is being termed the "trickle-up effect." In real terms, effective school-based civics education programs are bringing parents to the polls, teaching civic responsibility to children and engendering political interest among previously disengaged citizens — both young and old.

So you're probably reading this and wondering why these programs don't already exist in every county of every state. You might even remember taking a civics course (remarkably, mine was called Participation in Government, and affectionately coined "PIG") and expect that all American students go through similar courses in high school. Sadly, these programs don't exist in enough places around the nation. And worse, according to a study by the Representative Democracy in America Project, adults throughout the past 50 years have stopped passing on their civic knowledge and stressing the importance of being engaged and involved to young people.

The results of this failure to pass along information are evident in the civic action (or inaction) and attitudes of young people. Researchers surveyed 15 to 26 year-olds throughout America and found that only 66 percent believe that voting is a requirement for being a "good citizen." This figure starkly contrasts to the 83 percent of respondents older than 26 who felt it was important. About half of people 26 or younger regularly follow news about government, contrasted with three-fourths of those 26 years of age or older.

This study reinforces the notion that civic education programs are sorely needed and must proliferate in the coming years. Roughly 71 percent of young people who had taken a civics course believed voting to be an important component of citizenship. Further, young people who took a civics class were two to three times more likely than those who didn't, not only to vote, but also to stay informed about government activity and contact elected officials about issues that matter to them. Currently, 39 states require students to participate in some sort of civics program before graduation. But these courses usually do not go far enough. As outlined at the start of this chapter, voting is a habit that must be taught early and reinforced over time if it is to be a part of peoples' perceived duty as good citizens.

So how do we go about making civics courses a more prevalent and valued part of the American education system? American teachers already face the daunting task of finding the time to incorporate volumes of curriculum requirements into their daily lectures and classroom activities. The answer is not the introduction of a new civics course into each year of schooling (although that would be ideal). It's just not practical with all that is already expected of teachers. Instead, state and local governments should find ways to weave pieces of civic education into every component and subject area of their curriculum, in each grade, each year.

Additional steps to remedy the civic education deficit should include:

- Dedicating a section of school system Web sites to the housing of a year-long curriculum replete with lesson plans and classroom activities. Teachers can use this resource when needed and as time allows. The site should also include a section with non-partisan information on political candidates, the electoral process, community service programs and other tools to excite students about the civic process.
- School systems should build alliances with local community and civic organizations like 100 Black Men, The League of Women Voters, Boys and Girl Scouts of America, etc., to develop programs and vehicles that continue the civic education program beyond the classroom and into everyday life. This should include "education kits," containing civic activities and lesson plans that work in concert with school curriculums and reinforce the messages gleaned from classroom activities.

- Peer leadership should be harnessed in order to engender a sense of civic responsibility in America's youth. This peer team concept is similar to many other student organizations already in existence, like Students Against Drunk Driving, the National Honor Society and the Christian Athletic Council.

As evidenced throughout this book, citizens face numerous barriers to civic participation and a cadre of other, more interesting or demanding activities that make being involved less meaningful. Civic education programs play a vital role in building a basic understanding of the process and a passion and commitment to being involved. Used in concert, these techniques should plant the seeds for a desire to take part that overcomes many of the obstacles that limit active citizenship for so many Americans.

Chapter 12

The Civic Tri-Axiom: Personal Barriers

Finally, the last leg of the Civic Tri-Axiom — people do not participate in the civic process for a host of personal reasons and life factors that are compounded by the barriers listed previously in this section of the book. The personal barriers are perhaps the most difficult to overcome because they deal with the manner in which Americans go about their daily lives.

As we'll see, Americans today work more, spend less time with family and generally have less time to engage in things outside of the immediate necessities of life. Personal barriers, perhaps more than the other two legs of the tri-axiom, explain why Americans vote less, fail to join community organizations, distrust their neighbors, government and communities and participate less in sports or other social networking.

This section will also investigate another barrier that until recently has received relatively limited blame for diminishing civic participation — technology's grip on our time. To understand why people are less engaged in the civic process, this chapter will examine the personal barrier from two perspectives: The harried life for most families and citizens in the 21ˢᵗ Century; and the negative impact of technology — particularly television and the Internet — on active involvement.

American Life in the 21ˢᵗ Century

We learned in the last chapter that elder family members do not take time to pass along the importance of participating in the civic process. And schools aren't doing enough to fill the void. Hence, younger generations have a weakened sense of civic responsibility. For young and old Americans, civic participation takes a back seat to other, more valued or necessary activities. So as American quality of life changes and becomes more hectic, engagement in government and community activity falls by the wayside. American life in the late 20ᵗʰ and early 21ˢᵗ centuries moves at a frenetic pace. According to a survey in the late 1990s, the number of Americans who "always" feel rushed *doubled* from similar poll responses in the 1960s.

Currently, Americans work more than people in any other nation in the industrialized world. The typical American also takes less vacation time, works longer days and basks in the glow of retirement at a much later age. Figures from the Bureau of Labor Statistics show that the typical worker spent an increasing number of hours on the job each year during the 1990s. The figure peaked within the past few years, and now rests at just more than 40 hours per week. When all the extra hours were added up, Americans were working the equivalent of an additional month per year in 1990 compared to 1970.

In 1999, more than 25 million Americans — nearly 20.5 percent of the entire workforce — reported spending at least 49 hours per week on the job. About 11 million of those people said they worked more than 59 hours each week. As all of us average hard-working Americans know, all this time on the job leads to feelings of stress, being overworked and rushed in all aspects of life. The results are obvious and palpable: recent phenomena like road rage, workplace violence, expanding daycare rolls and the increased existence of after-school programming that serves as caretakers for America's youth.

More recently, a 2003 poll found that roughly 26 percent of Americans feel overworked. That seems like a relatively small percentage of the population — only a quarter. But that is double the number of people (13 percent) who felt the same way in a 1960 survey. And this feeling rises when kids join the family unit: one-third of Americans with kids feel overworked.

Additional life factors like traffic congestion sap remaining time and energy. In cities across the nation, traffic congestion continues to worsen. In 2001, the average American spent nearly 50 minutes each day driving to and from work.

So why are Americans working so much? A good place to start is with a picture of how Americans see themselves and the things they value. A recent *Reader's Digest* and Gallup Organization study found that most people see four factors critical to personal well-being. In ranking order, they are: financial security, health and healthcare, family and personal relationships, and community issues. This study sheds light on a picture of Americans who work longer hours to make ends meet or to pay off escalating personal debt.

At the end of the day, after dealing with the rigors of work, battling traffic and completing other necessary personal tasks, Americans are tired and in need of peace, quiet and time alone. As a result, engaging in family activities and personal pursuits takes on secondary importance, leaving community and civic engagement at the end of "to-do" lists.

Women: "You've come a long way baby!"

Clearly, life has changed significantly for women during the past 40 years. Between the 1950s and the late 1970s, a significant number of American women stayed home to care for their families, and many of them spent significant time in social and civic pursuits. Stay-at-home moms made our communities hum by joining the PTA and neighborhood or church groups. In addition to the full-time job of raising a family, these women saw to it that the larger community's needs were met as well.

America is obviously a better place now that we have the vision, talent and drive of women in the workforce and in positions of leadership. But it has left a real void in the proliferation and success of civic organizations and community activity.

Recent studies chronicle the decline in American civic participation. Organizational membership for men has declined at about 10 percent to 15 percent per decade, but women have stopped joining groups at a rate of about 20 percent to 25 percent per decade. Working women tend to volunteer or "join" more regularly than housewives. However, the stay-at-home set, tend to provide more hours to the organizations they participate in. On the surface, this seems like a paradox — but it's not. In simple terms, a significant portion of women entering the workforce during the past few decades were formerly the most active housewives and those who took leadership positions in their civic activities.

Now, the most active women — those more likely to exemplify leadership traits — are joining more personally-focused organizations. They join groups based on the level of opportunity for personal development and career advancement. Community and more civic-based organizations take the brunt of this shift, and as a result, have suffered from smaller membership rolls and fewer tangible outputs.

The Family Crunch

The decline in interest and time for American families to participate in the civic process is particularly problematic because it requires that married couples become more active to offset the disengagement and cynicism of an expanding class of single people. The number of one-person households has nearly doubled since 1950. And the proportion of unmarried adult Americans has risen from 28 percent in 1974 to 48 percent in 1994.

Not surprisingly, single people (divorced, never married or separated men and women) are significantly less trusting and less civically engaged than "coupled" Americans. Married people are about a third more trusting and belong to 15 percent to 25 percent more civic organizations than single people. Statistically speaking, married people, particularly those with children are more trusting and engaged. And as a result, they are forced to carry a larger burden of civic activity. That is unless we can change the attitudes and behavior of a significant segment of the population.

So how successful are America's married people at carrying the civic burden, so to speak? In short: Not very. Married people, particularly those with children, might be more civically active than single people but are not making the time to engage. Marriage and family demands limit the time for civic pursuits in two ways: increased financial burdens and elevated demand on free time. Marriage traditionally brings added financial burdens, particularly when children are born. According to the *Reader's Digest* poll mentioned earlier, nearly 33 percent of American families claim to be in moderate to heavy debt. And 47 percent find it difficult to pay for healthcare. As a result, these increased financial burdens tend to require both spouses to work. More than 78 percent of married people have a spouse that also works. That is a significant rise from the 66 percent of people in the same boat 20 years ago.

As a result, paid work takes priority over things like eating meals together, getting children ready for school and other household chores. These tasks get left for the weekend or after long days in the office. As evidence, about 38 percent of Americans say they don't spend enough time with their families.

Personal time, including socializing, community activity, voting, sports, etc. are the first things to get cut from the routine when people spend more time in the office. Today, mothers take less than an hour a day for personal activities. That's 42 minutes less than the time spent 20 years ago. Fathers spend a bit more than an hour each day on personal activities, which is roughly 54 minutes less than 20 years ago. While two jobs make paying the bills and buying the trappings of the 21st century easier, the dual income trend is taking its toll on civic America.

Role of Technology

The barriers to participation discussed above are significant. But they pale in comparison to the monster of civic decline that has remained hidden until recently. One of America's foremost experts on civic participation, Robert Putnam, recently articulated perhaps the most significant barrier — *the proliferation of television*. The following section will examine TV's role in reducing trust in government and lessening the amount of free time available to join and participate. We'll also take a closer look at whether the Internet has the potential to produce the same negative impact TV has on civic participation, or can become a participatory elixir.

Why is TV to blame? According to Putnam, we must return to an examination of the Greatest Generation to more clearly understand TV's role in American civic decline. We know that generation was the most civically active in American history. No set of people was as engaged previously or since. What's most interesting and led Putnam to his conclusion is that they were the last generation to grow up without TV as a significant influencer.

The television first entered American households following the conclusion of World War II. Only 10 percent of households owned one in 1950. In an amazing instance of unprecedented technological growth, nearly 90 percent of households had a television by 1960. As TV's prevalence grew, so did America's proclivity for spending time on the couch in front of it. The number of hours people spent glued to the tube jumped by nearly 20 percent in the 1960s. And it rose another seven to eight percent in the 1970s. And the amount of time an average American spent watching television was nearly 50 percent higher in 1995 than it was in 1950. That's one of the most staggering rises of technology immersion in world history.

Today, the average American watches nearly four hours of TV per day. On the surface, that doesn't seem like a significant amount of time. But remember that Americans today have a limited amount of free time because of their increased workloads, family pressures, commutes and other life factors. Now add four hours of TV viewing to the mix. No wonder civic participation is dropping precipitously in recent decades. According to current studies, TV takes up nearly 40 percent of people's free time, which is a staggering one-third increase from 1965.

Watching TV was a family affair in the 1950s. People gathered to watch Ed Sullivan and a host of other programs geared towards all segments of the household. You could flip on the tube and hear songs by Bing Crosby or the Beatles and jokes by Milton Berle and Henny

Youngman. But as time passed, and with the advent of cable television, the types and number of channels exploded. Before, Americans had a limited number of stations and programs to choose from at any one time. But now people can turn to a channel to see the latest news, flip to another to watch sports or find a cadre of other programming among an increasingly long list of options. During the same timeframe, TVs became more advanced, cheaper, and as a result, more ubiquitous. More than 75 percent of all U.S. households had multiple TVs by the late 1980s. As a result, family members dispersed to separate rooms throughout the house to enjoy their program of choice. Just think about life in your own home: Do you have a TV in your bedroom, living room and/or library — or even the kitchen? At night, is there one family member in each room watching a different program? This change in the way people spend their free time directly correlates to the decline in civic engagement.

But the negative effects of TV aren't just associated with the amount of free time people give up to tune in. TV also has a negative impact on people's social trust and cynicism. Social capital is a measure of people's connectedness to their communities. TV produces low social capital because it reduces social trust and connectedness to groups. And over time, heavy TV viewers are likely to become "loners." A recent study found that 40 percent of Americans are highly concerned about the negative impact TV watching is having on the members of their immediate family. In very real terms, each hour spent watching television correlates to one less hour spent investing in social capital.

Obviously, there are a multitude of things that led to America's decreased civic participation throughout history — many of them have been discussed already in this section of the book. But it is no coincidence that the rise in TV watching tracks the decline in American civic participation during the last 50 years. It is no exaggeration then to assume that the rise of TV bears a significant brunt of the responsibility for people spending less time engaged in civic America.

What does this mean for future generations? Currently, the average American child spends more than 40 hours per week glued to a television set. That's 40 hours, a full work-week for most adults. For young children, those nine to 14 years old, TV takes up as much time as all other activities combined. It replaces playing sports, joining clubs, engaging in hobbies, outdoor activities and other informal social interaction. Studies also show that heavy viewing among young people increases aggressiveness, distrust, cynicism and general laziness — all leading to decreased social capital and overall civic engagement.

Americans have grown tired of hearing negative prognostications of the future. While incredibly cynical as a society, we hold an underlying belief that as a nation, we can overcome any obstacle and tackle any problem. But just look at the facts: Adding TV consumption to the multitude of civic barriers is a recipe for disaster. Unless our viewing habits change soon, the future of civic participation is in serious jeopardy.

The Internet: Civic Savior or TV Clone?

At its introduction to society, many experts believed television offered an enormous opportunity to positively shape America's social fabric, expanding culture and uniting a national community. And now, another technological wonder has offered similar opportunities — personal computers and the Internet. The availability and rapid deployment of the Internet has paralleled TV's growth. Many Internet proponents believe it holds the keys to linking people in ways never before imagined. This interconnectivity is believed to hold the future of global communities by connecting people regardless of time zone, distance or language.

The technology is in its relative infancy, and its impact won't be determined for decades — or perhaps generations — to come. But we can use TV's legacy as a guide to understand the Internet's potential opportunities and challenges. Will it bring us together or further pull us apart?

The Rise of the Internet

It is difficult to definitively state at this point what kind of impact the Internet will have on American society since the technology is so new and still gaining momentum. However, by 1998, personal computers existed in nearly 40 percent of all U.S. households. And one-third of these computer owners had access to the Internet. Again, like television, computers and the Internet have followed a meteoric path to social acceptance and personal use.

A recent study of the Internet's impact by the Stanford Institute for the Quantitative Study of Society showed that Americans are indeed spending more time "online" as the technology grows, and less time with family, friends and pursuing activities in the "real world." As you'd expect, the more time people spend online or interacting with their computer, the less time they spend engaging with other human beings. Specifically, the folks at Stanford found that:

- The time spent online grows relative to the number of years people have had access to a personal computer.
- Nearly 25 percent of active Internet users (those spending more than five hours a week online) believe they are now spending

less time with family and friends and less time outside their office or home.

- Technology has made work a more prevalent part of our lives. Nearly 25 percent of employed Internet users say that this technology has increased the amount of hours they work at home, without a reduction of time in the office. Perhaps this is true because the Internet has also cut efficiency at the office.
- It appears that the Internet is actually replacing TV in people's lives. Nearly 60 percent of regular Internet users say they now spend less time watching TV, and one-third say they read the newspaper less.

But while the Internet replaces TV viewing to an extent, it also takes away from time people spend interacting face-to-face with other humans or chatting on the phone.

Some experts take a contrarian viewpoint, arguing that the Internet actually increases social interaction because so many of its users spend time e-mailing friends, family members, neighbors and even people around the world. But the Internet experience doesn't provide the same kind of personal interaction that takes place in the real world. You can't send a hug to someone having a bad day via e-mail. Think about it. Has someone sent you an animated greeting card to brighten your day? If so, did it have the same effect as a personally written greeting card or a warm smile? Or did it just feel like another piece of spam in your inbox?

According to Stanford professor Norman Nie, who ran the study, "The Internet could be the ultimate isolating technology that further reduces our participation in communities even more than did automobiles and television before it." Professor Nie is ultimately driving the point that the Internet is something people utilize alone. It's not like TV, which can be left on as background noise, taking little of our direct attention. Surfing the web or sending an e-mail is not a passive activity and requires immediate attention and activity.

Proponents of the Internet see chat rooms, texting, Web logs (blogs) and other interactive online tools as the keys to uniting people and building bridges between distant communities. Unfortunately, it appears that the majority of Internet usage is people sending e-mails to individuals that they already know or surfing for information. Typical bloggers or chat room attendees are less than 30 years old, and their use is only now appearing to grow.

Specifically, a majority of active Internet surfers use it as a consumer resource and spend their time seeking information. More than 50 percent of these people say they use the Web for travel and product information. And more than one-third of Internet users admit to buying products online, and as a result, spending less time in brick-and-mortar stores interacting with salespeople and other consumers.

We could draft entire chapters and even books on the recent phenomenon of Internet dating and online communities like myspace and facebook. These sites do indeed assist strangers in getting acquainted, and in thousands of cases, actually lead to long-term relationships. And in others, these sites assist people in promoting their bands, selling goods and services and connecting with strangers for positive (and sometimes "casual") purposes.

However, there appears to be a dangerous and negative underbelly to myspace and other online communities. Federal, state and local law enforcement agencies are actively pursuing child pornographers and other despicable individuals who prey on minors, the weak and naïve. And perhaps most tragically, a recent string of school shootings seems to be driven by connections made on the Internet.

The Internet and new Web services are making it easier for people to connect for a range of purposes. But is that a good thing? And how does all this impact our personal relationships, trust and engagement in the community at-large? Early indications are that the Internet is diminishing our civic and social interactions even though its social aspects arguably had a more positive effect than television viewing. The reason is that the Internet regularly, if loosely, connects people via e-mail, chat rooms and other tools.

But strong interpersonal relationships typically require close proximity and nurturing. The Internet does not allow for this, and in the end, encourages weaker relationships. And again, as mentioned above, it diminishes our free time to build meaningful human, face-to-face relationships.

Recent studies show that increased Internet usage did indeed decrease the amount of time families spend playing together, eating as a group or finishing household chores. The Stanford study found that greater utilization of the Internet led to a weakening in strength and diminishing in size of local and distant social circles. They also found that people using the Internet reported increased feelings of loneliness. Alarmingly, the study actually found instances of increased depression among heavy Internet users, and this isn't surprising if you think about it. Stress tends to be a precursor, or in some cases, a root cause of depression. And it is social interaction — spending time with family and friends, getting that hug, smile or pat on the back — that helps hold depression at bay.

Much like television, it appears Internet usage leads to diminished social and civic interaction. As a result, we need to be cognizant of our time spent online, as it is likely to negatively impact our civic process — adding to democracy's decline. Only time will tell, but we should take precautionary steps to ensure that we don't lose future generations to some of the passive, isolating activities associated with the Internet and video games.

Impacts on Voting

Voting is one of the central pillars of American civic engagement. Evidence outlined above seems to contradict the opinion of some experts who predict that the Internet has the potential to revolutionize politics in the 21st century. The belief is that this medium of communication provides citizens with grassroots networking capabilities and access to non-partisan and unbiased candidate and issue information on a scale previously unknown.

Adding up what we've just learned, people fail to vote for a host of personal reasons beyond institutional obstacles. Quite simply, many Americans feel the inconvenience of voting far outweighs the impact their one vote will have on an election's outcome. Another major obstacle to electoral involvement for countless Americans is access to untarnished, unbiased candidate and issue information. Study after study shows that people don't know where to find detailed information on issues and candidates. And oftentimes, what they do see is personal candidate attack advertising and "mudslinging politics."

Technology proponents stress that now, Americans can simply flip on TV or hop online to find an array of information about issues, candidates and elections. According to these experts, the Internet provides an extensive and diverse collection of information and viewpoints to help them choose how to vote. But, ironically, in some cases, it's the availability of an abundance of information that causes a problem. In other words, there is so much content available that people are bombarded with white noise.

For all of the Internet's inherent merit, it is becoming increasingly full of content that limits people's access to information they truly trust and value. And so, this potentially powerful education resource gets lumped into the pile of TV and radio campaign spots and other information that people don't trust or have time to consider thoroughly. Or the content is more sizzle than substance. For confirmation, see the rise of Youtube candidate spoofs and videos dedicated to "how hot" Barack Obama actually is!

Research shows many American voters, particularly the young, are insecure about "making the wrong choice" because they do not have enough information to make an informed decision. Voters are faced with countless choices on the ballot, and they are expected to knowledgeably elect the candidate that best represents their interests. Not only do people have to vote for president, congress and state representatives, they must also cast ballots for judges, county commissioners and issue referendums. These often-complex issues contain little explanation on the ballot and are covered minimally in the media.

Information is constantly at our finger tips whether on 24-hour television, talk radio or the Internet. But it builds into a crescendo of white nose that ultimately leaves people less informed, or at least less inclined to wade through the growing piles of data. Finding trustworthy and substantive information becomes a challenge with less governed media like the Internet serving as free-for-all forums where anyone can voice an opinion. This is increasingly true with blogs or places like Wikepedia.com whose content is not guided by "fact" but approval of the online "community."

Subsequently, Americans are expected to figure out how to effectively navigate this vast, foreign ocean of knowledge to mine trusted and illuminating information. In many cases, this leads to increased costs to the individual and more barriers to electoral participation. These personal roadblocks maintain and increase voter apathy and disengagement.

Campaign Politics and the Internet's Promise

Some political experts see the Internet as the tool for leveling the political playing field. Candidates are able to make information available to voters without the negative and distorted filters associated with traditional campaign ads. And voters no longer have to decide who to cast ballots for based solely on 30-second TV ads. They can go to a candidate's Web site and learn about their background, experience, platform and voting record.

Perhaps the 2004 election and the surprising early success of former Vermont Governor Howard Dean supported this line of reasoning. Dean's campaign provides some interesting lessons, even though he was unable to harness the power of Internet activity to win the Democratic Party's nomination — or even get active online supporters to volunteer or follow through with a vote in 2004. Howard Dean used the Internet to move from obscure northeast governor to Democratic front-runner almost overnight. Dean's campaign was the most successful at using the power of the Internet to get unparalleled access to people's ideas, social networks and wallets. In a short time, he raised millions of dollars and recruited thousands of volunteers online. Consider the facts:

- In the second quarter of 2003, Dean claimed to have raised more than $3.5 million of his $7.5 million total from online contributors.
- Dean was able to arrange rallies and volunteer events in more than 400 cities on June 23, 2003, to coincide with the announcement of his candidacy.
- Dean raised more than $7.4 million dollars online in the third quarter of 2003. In an astonishing break from political cam-

paign norms, he raised the money in small chunks, not from huge individual and corporate gifts (which are now banned by the McCain-Feingold Act signed into law in 2003). The third quarter windfall was culled from 110,786 online contributions by 84,713 individual supporters at an average rate of $61.14.

- And by late 2003, he used Meetup.com, a recently developed grassroots campaign phenomenon, to recruit more than 61,000 volunteers.

But Dean for America was not the first campaign to utilize the power of the Internet for recruiting voters, volunteers and raising large sums of money. He was just the most effective to that point. Here's a brief history of the Internet and politics:

- Jerry Brown, a Democratic candidate for President in 1992, was the first to use e-mail in a political campaign.
- Sen. Dianne Feinstein (D-CA) launched the first campaign Web site in 1994.
- Jesse Ventura, the former pro-wrestler and one-time governor of Minnesota, is widely held as the first candidate to win an election because of the Internet.
- Bill Bradley was the first candidate to raise $1 million on-line when he ran for the Democratic presidential nomination in 2000.
- Sen. John McCain's 2000 campaign for president was the first to raise $500,000 online in *one day*.
- And during the 2000 election, the Republican Party was the first to register one million online activists.

So how exactly have campaigns been using the Internet to gain support and win elections? Initially, it was used as a source of basic information. Candidates saw it as a way to provide significant details about their backgrounds and proposals that weren't subject to either the scrutiny of media or distortion by their opponents. They could carefully craft and deliver messages and a persona that fit their campaign and wasn't shaped by others. It's sort of like writing on the chalkboard before anyone else does. And that means you have to spend less time going back to erase the image or "distortions" crafted by others.

From there, as outlined above, candidates began using the Internet as a tool for organizing campaign supporters and volunteers. Internet activity has evolved to a point today where online organizing, fundraising, e-mail lists and volunteer recruitment are essential, basic elements of running a political campaign.

But Governor Dean incorporated the Internet into his campaign in a manner unlike any candidate in history. Volunteers were recruited online to make phone calls, send letters to voters in the early primary states and other activities. Additionally, he raised significant amounts of money and recruited record levels of volunteers from every corner of our nation and around the world without the need for face-to-face interaction. His site even provided technology-savvy supporters with an electronic world of information and connectivity via cell phone and Blackberry campaign updates, "blogs," and an online chain of personal communications. These seem like simple technological tools today, but they were political innovations only a few short years ago.

It is Dean's early success that forced Internet skeptics, campaign consultants, candidates and others to stand up and take notice. Politicians and their campaigns tend to stick to the tried and true tactics. Most political campaigns possess the ability to identify the key or "swing" voters living in their district needed to win an election. And they usually have a clear understanding of the voters and supporters already in their camp.

Furthermore, they know the tactics and campaign tools that will get these people to support them and the messages that will win converts. New campaign techniques are adopted over time and only after other candidates have worked out the bugs first. Dean's early successes provided other candidates with a blueprint for navigating this new technology, and the comfort to test it for their own ends. Technological innovation is becoming a critical role for all presidential campaigns — more on that to come.

Governor Dean successfully secured small, individual donations from a broader base of supporters to compete with the "real world" fundraising of a sitting president who was appealing to the usual, big individual and corporate donor types. A prime example comes from early 2003. Vice President Dick Cheney was scheduled to keynote a fundraiser in South Carolina that would cull money from the traditional big donor crowd. Governor Dean called upon his online supporters to outgive the high-dollar contributors at Cheney's "real world" event. And in a mere three days, Dean for America raised more than $500,000 online from this one request — nearly twice the amount raised at Vice President Cheney's event.

It is this type of success that helps donors and volunteers, many of whom feel disconnected from politics and politicians, to become invested in something bigger than their own daily worlds. Dean's new online recruits gave of their time, their money and their thoughts. Dean for America staff actually sifted through the thousands of e-mails and blogs for tips, ideas or suggestions that would give them the edge in 2004. One of Governor Dean's most popular slogans, "people-powered Howard," actually came from an online supporter.

Dean went where few candidates had gone before: He ran a race "of the people," by turning a measure of power and decision-making over *to the people.* And it initially appeared to be amazingly successful, at least in the early stages, prior to the actual casting of votes. But as outlined in previous chapters, the Internet is a conundrum of connectivity. It provides people with information and forums for social interaction. But the information can get cluttered, and the resulting social networks tend to be built upon weak, relatively "real-world-passive" relationships.

Governor Dean seemed to initially prove the Internet's proponents right in that people's solitary surfing led to a windfall of financial contributions and inter-connected campaign activity. As was the case with Jesse Ventura during his run for Minnesota governor, many of Dean's online supporters were first-time volunteers and voters. Sure, some of these folks were the stalwarts of liberal Democratic politics who tend to be tech savvy, politically astute and engaged regardless of the medium. But many of these supporters were people traditionally turned-off by politics and disengaged from the larger civic process.

Early in the election, it appeared that the Internet might be allowing candidates to connect with people in very personal and meaningful ways. As we'll see in the case studies section of this book, it is this personal connection — making government and candidates seem more real and impactful — that is critical to moving people to civic action. Yet the jury is still out on whether this online activity and enthusiasm can translate into real world votes — and if the mouse clicking that led to so much money and momentum for Dean can translate to the real shuffling of feet to the polls and the casting of votes.

One explanation for the demise of Governor Dean's campaign (long before the "scream heard round the world") was the failure of converting online activists into real world volunteers, surrogates, organizers and voters. Only time and closer scrutiny will truly uncover whether Dean's early success was inflated by online activity that didn't require real-world actions, like casting a vote. Donating money online, sharing candidate information with friends and other Internet-driven activities take less commitment than actually going to the polls. And there is far less accountability since the actions don't require actual human interaction. For instance, going online, typing in a credit card number and hitting send is very different from visiting a campaign office and giving cash or a check. There isn't a real person on the other end of that gift to say thank you or ask you to do more.

Dean's meteoric rise led many to believe that a new day in politics had arrived. One where the Internet could be a great force for leveling the political playing field, giving rise to the voices of America's great, disaffected masses. In fact, Dean's candidacy sent a chill into the staid political arena. Fear arose in certain circles that outsiders and political neophytes were storming the gates and demanding power.

But ultimately, Dean wasn't successful, and it will be some time before future political candidates rely solely on the technological tools of the Dean machine. They will never replace the benefits of shaking a hand, kissing a baby or looking a big donor in the face and asking for more. Instead, most will continue to use the staid tricks of the trade as the core of their operations. New technologies are created every day — cameras get smaller, communication channels more pervasive and information sharing more omnipresent. And campaigns will continue to test and bring on new technologies. However, the true impact of technology on connecting people and turning out actual voters will take some time to become clear. And in the end, we'll have to wait to see if the Internet holds the promise for a more connected America or is the cause of participation's further decline.

The 2006 and 2008 elections continue to provide similarly contradictory information on the future of Internet activity in the political world. Yes, the technology continues to grow in stature among campaign toolboxes. The 2006 elections provide a great case study for the continued rise of the Internet as a tool for reaching voters and donors.

The drag of the Iraq war, political scandals among Republican legislators and a host of issues brought America's focus beaming on the 2006 midterm election like a laser-guided bomb. As a result, the Democratic Party anticipated an opportunity to seize power in both chambers of Congress. And both the party apparatus and grassroots activists suited up for battle. The Internet would prove to be one of the chief weapons in the grassroots arsenal. And for us and this book, we found another chance to gauge the potential of technology in the civic world.

Howard Dean had moved from failed presidential candidate to head of the Democratic National Committee. In large measure, he took control of the office through the support of the liberal wing of the party. These supporters tend to be highly educated, computer-literate and engaged more than average Democrats and Americans. Dean used this power to build a "50-state strategy" that would see the party placing resources in all states, not just those that were winnable come election time. This was a departure from the established Democratic playbook and was an effort to replicate the deep bench that Republicans had successfully stocked during the past two decades.

About the same time, a new power base arose within the party — the "netroots." The term refers to people using the Internet to educate and mobilize political activists. These activists tend to be some of the most liberal in the Democratic Party. And many were previously not active participants in the political process at all. They disdained government and turned away because their voices were rarely heard by politicians "cozying up" to lobbyists and special interests. Netroots certainly weren't seen as party insiders. They used the Internet to give voice to dissatisfaction with the current course of the party, and its leaders' willingness to compromise with Republicans. And the resulting army of bloggers expressed their extreme anger over the Democratic Party's inability to bring the troops home.

Many of the netroot leaders and organizations found their start in the Dean machine. A growing group of Internet celebrities began to spring up because they understood new communication channels, like blogs. Organizations such as MoveOn.org and individuals like Markos Moulitsas Zuniga (Dailykos.com) and Jerome Armstrong found a place to rant against current government policies and the direction of the war in Iraq. But interestingly, they used these new technologies and their growing voice to attack leaders in their own party for not being liberal enough. And God save anyone who voted for a Republican-led bill or spoke out in favor of something President Bush proposed. These treasonous acts would be reported and maligned in real-time and known by thousands of people almost instantly.

There are many good books on the rise of this netroot movement. For our purposes, it's most important to know that this group was gaining a voice within the party and sought to test their power in the 2006 election. Senator Joe Lieberman (D-CT), a darling of the party only a few years before, became the recipient of the netroot vitriol and angst. A movement sought to throw him out of Congress for standing with President Bush and the Republicans on the war in Iraq. They found their champion in millionaire communications mogul Ned Lamont who agreed to take on Lieberman in the primary election. Lamont got off to a slow start, struggling with the typical apparatus needed to run a successful political campaign. But an infusion of millions from his own bank account and support from bloggers and groups like MoveOn.org assisted in making the election a real contest. And ultimately, Ned Lamont won the Democratic primary and was the party's candidate for the general election. This was a bitter contest, pitting party stalwarts and residents of Connecticut against political neophytes and liberal, angry online activists.

Senator Lieberman was clearly blindsided by the attack from his own party and the resulting, unceremonious ouster. Yet he rebounded and vowed to fight. This time, he rejoined the battle as an independent candidate in the general election. Let's pause to consider what happened here. An extremely liberal faction of the Democratic Party sought to flex their collective muscles. And found a primary battle where they could send a message to the Democratic establishment: "Ignore us, and our causes at your own peril." This group was led by well-funded Democrats, many of whom began to spend their wealth on politics for the first time. And interestingly, technology was used as the driving force for recruiting volunteers, raising money for candidates — Lamont in this instance — and educating potential voters about the "treachery" of Joe Lieberman. These new netroots led similar charges in campaigns across America. But the Lieberman contest was the height of their power during the 2006 elections.

The General Election results lead us to an interesting crossroads for where we are with technology's role in modern American politics. Much like 2004 and Dean's meteoric rise to power, the Internet provided disgruntled or previously marginalized people with a voice in the political process. They found others, shared information and took action in a multitude of manners. They made a lot of noise. But as we saw in the General Election, this fury ultimately signified nothing. Many of these political outsiders were unable to vote. The Internet allowed them to stir the pot and bring people out for the Democratic primary. But they weren't on the ground in Connecticut, and they weren't residents, eligible to vote. As a result, Ned Lamont and a Republican also-ran lost to Joe Lieberman, who retained his seat. But now, he was an Independent member of the U.S. Senate. This ultimately freed him from toting the Democratic line. And the irony is fairly obvious — these partisan, vitriolic Democrats storming the gates actually weakened the party. They lost an almost-certain Democratic seat, and a strong voice in the Senate. Let's keep in mind that Senator Lieberman was the party's vice presidential candidate a mere two years earlier.

Ultimately, the 2006 elections and this one case study, continue to muddy the waters of the Internet's ultimate political power. Evolving technologies empowered a new pool of political players. And they used their voice to make waves within their party. But ultimately, they failed to meet the goal of ousting Joe Lieberman. Sure, there were numerous factors besides those articulated above, that led to the ultimate outcome. But it's clear that the Internet alone, isn't enough to build the inevitable revolution many people claim to be heading our way.

Instead, the Internet is becoming a reliable tool for candidates and their campaigns. Its uses are valuable; much like direct mail pieces or "robo calling" (automated phone calls to likely voters). But the Internet is no silver bullet or nuclear option for revolutionizing politics and the way we run campaigns that ensure strong voter turnout and victory on Election Day.

The 2008 campaign provides yet another opportunity to evaluate the power of this less-new arrow in the political quiver. The current presidential election received more attention from average citizens at an earlier time than ever before. Perhaps that speaks to the gravity of this election and the world-altering issues at stake. But candidates are continuing to embrace the Internet, blogs and evolving technologies. And it is endearing them to potential donors, volunteers and voters.

Congressman Ron Paul is a perfect example, as he seems to be the Republican version of Howard Dean in 2004. Ultimately, he is winning ardent fans and altered the discourse in the primary. But his chances for victory were slim.

And so, the Internet continues to play a powerful role in elections. But it's unlikely that it will empower one candidate to victory and be *the* factor that locks up the election. We will have to monitor the outcome. But the result is certain. The Internet is not the silver bullet for restoring "a government of the people, by the people, and for the people."

Chapter 13

Conclusion

America is on a slippery slope of civic participation. Our most active citizens tend to be our oldest, and the generations of Americans taking their place are facing increasingly demanding lifestyles that limit time for, and interest in, active civic participation. These citizens also lack the basic grounding principles of civic activism that should have been taught early in life and reinforced through ongoing awareness and participation. Add the draining draw of TV and the Internet to the mix, and you have the potential for catastrophically low levels of civic participation in years to come.

Well, we've gotten some of the bad news out of the way. We've seen the declining levels of America's civic engagement, and we have a better handle on the root causes. The good news is that hope exists. We can have a more vibrant and engaged America — one where citizens not only volunteer at the local level to tackle problems in their communities. But one where they add ideas and voices to the policy debates filling the halls of government in county seats and in the nation's capitals.

The next section of this book is devoted to previous organizational efforts to improve civic participation and examples of what worked and what did not. The things that weren't successful will serve as warnings for what not to replicate when trying to tackle America's civic decline. The efforts that were successful provide tools and lessons for future programs and initiatives.

Finally, the last section of this book presents real world case studies that show what works, the tools for engaging people and the issues that matter to Americans. And I hope, these examples will provide some insight into what inspires people to take civic action. Our challenge is real and significant. But we needn't pack it in and call it a day just yet. We shouldn't be ringing the death knell of our great nation, like Paul Revere in his famous ride through Colonial New England. But in order to be successful, we must learn from the past while moving forward with the tools of success and optimism that positive change is possible, even inevitable, if we work together and understand that legislation happens. It's just a question of whether it happens with, or to us.

Section IV

Chapters 14 – 17

Rebuilding Civic Participation: Previous Efforts.

Chapter 14

Introduction

Countless organizations have developed over time in America to encourage active civic participation. The reasons for the groups' genesis and their membership have varied by location, gender and race. Inevitably though, each was born from an issue or concern, like the Suffragettes who sought to bring equality to American women through the right to vote; the Student Nonviolent Coordinating Committee (SNCC), which sprung up during the Civil Rights movement to ensure the equitable treatment of African Americans; or the Human Rights Campaign, which fights for the equality of gays and lesbians across the nation today.

These organizations share several common characteristics: They seek to increase awareness for their cause, conduct public education, register people to vote and try to influence public policy though grass-roots organizing. While the groups vary in their specific tactics and goals, they share the common thread of trying to improve America through increased civic activity. As the prominence of groups with rich histories like the National Association for the Advancement of Colored People (NAACP), the League of Women Voters, labor unions and others faded, a new breed of organizations sprung up specifically focused on improving voter turnout.

A subtle shift in focus has taken place during the past few decades among the most prominent organizations working to increase voter turnout. In the '60s and '70s, activist organizations like SNCC and the NAACP used voter registration and mobilization *as a tool for reaching their desired goals* of racial and economic freedom, opportunity and equality. As we'll see in the following chapters, recently-created organizations are making the more visible pursuit of increased voter registration and turnout their *sole mission*. In other words, the tactics (getting people registered to vote) are more prominent and important at times than the larger goals or issues the organization might hope to address or remedy.

For instance, the record industry hoped active young voters would fight a CD rating system introduced by Congress that they deemed unfair and detrimental to their economic viability. But little education accompanied the registration efforts that would have armed young people for a legislative battle once out of the polls. As we'll see in future chapters, this is partly to blame for weak civic follow-through once increased numbers of voters are actually registered.

These new "mobilization" organizations have almost exclusively trained their efforts on America's youngest voters — those 18 to 24 (sometimes up to 30) years of age. This is particularly interesting since 18- to 24-year-olds, while the least-involved members in our electoral process, aren't alone in their civic negligence. Since 1974, citizens we'd consider adults of family-rearing years — those 25 to 44 — have failed as civic role models. Consider the following:

- 1996: Less than half of registered 25- to 44-year-olds voted.
- 1994: A mere 39.4 percent of 25- to 44-year-olds voted and only 56.7 percent of those 45 to 64

- 1986: A mere 41 percent of 25- to 44-year-olds voted.
- 1982: Roughly 45 percent of 25- to 44-year-olds voted, which is nearly 20 percent less than those 45 to 64 years of age
- 1974: Slightly more than 42 percent of 25- to 44-year-olds voted

In most cases since 1972, close to or slightly more than half of all 25 to 44 year-olds have voted in federal elections. While this is considerably higher participation than America's youngest voters, it is a lot less than the next two age brackets of voters tracked by the Federal Elections Commission. And as outlined in numerous sections of this book, the civic participation levels in America — the cradle of modern democracy — are less than percentages in numerous developing nations around the world. America has been engaged since September 11th, 2001 in a global conflict against terrorism that is based largely on efforts to advance democracy around the world. While America is truly the world leader on human rights and the treatment of people in general, we aren't global poster children for active voter turnout. Consider the numbers:

Nation	Year	Federal Elections Commission Turnout
Argentina	1995 Presidential	80.5
Azerbaijan	1993 Presidential	97.6
Brazil	1998 Presidential	78.52
Cameroon	1997 Presidential	81.35
Chile	1993 Presidential	90
Ecuador	1996 Presidential	73
Ghana	1996 Presidential	78.21

Nation	Year	Federal Elections Commission Turnout
Italy	1995 Regional	77.4
Kazakhstan	1999 Presidential	87.05
Moldova	1998 Parliamentary	86.6
Nicaragua	1996 Presidential	76.38
Panama	1999 Presidential	75.94
Tajikistan	1994 Presidential	89
Ukraine	1998 Parliamentary	86.6
U.S.A	**2000 Presidential**	**51.3**

The goal here is not to bash America's comparatively diminished voter turnout. The numbers highlight how, by failing to participate, Americans have come to take freedom for granted. The numbers simply and powerfully highlight the argument. While slightly more than 51 percent of Americans went to the polls in 1998 for legislative races, nearly 87 percent of Ukrainians and Moldavians did and almost 74 percent of people in the Czech Republic did as well. America's 51.3 percent turnout for the 2000 Presidential Election pales in comparison to the nearly 74 percent of Slovenians who participated in their parliamentary elections and the 68 percent of Russians who voted in their presidential elections.

Hopefully these striking figures hammer home the point that it isn't just young people who need to be brought back into the civic fold. And therefore, many of the mobilization organizations outlined above need to broaden their civic outreach efforts.

This section will examine some of the organizations that worked in the 1990s to improve youth voter participation. We'll identify their goals, tactics and achievements to illuminate what worked, as well as what was missing from these efforts. The first half of this book painted the bleak picture of where we stand in our national civic engagement. The following chapters will hopefully inspire people to paint a new picture of civic participation in the United States. The following chapters, which focus primarily on Rock the Vote and MTV's Choose or Lose campaign, will provide solid steps for engendering a sense of civic responsibility in America. This blueprint can lead to increased active engagement from potential voters of all ages and backgrounds.

Chapter 15

Organizations That Tried "Rocking the Vote"

The following chapters examine groups in the "National Youth Voter Registration Movement (NYVRM)." The NYVRM name clearly states the mission of these groups: to register young voters in the hopes of increasing overall participation in the American electoral process. The agendas of these groups aren't transparent like those outlined in this section's introduction. In fact, NYVRM groups appeared to be almost altruistic in nature, because they claimed to have no agenda other than creating a greater pool of voters.

Members of the NYVRM were very successful in registering young people to vote and in disseminating non-partisan candidate and issue information. However, with the exception of the 1992 presidential election, voter turnout did not coincide with increased numbers of registered young people. And as we'll see at the end of this book, the 2004 election represented the most massive undertaking of the NYVRM, and it too produced marginal results. A closer examination of the resulting disconnect between increased registration and stagnant or diminished voter turnout will provide tangible lessons for future efforts.

A continuous decline in youth voter participation since 1972 was the galvanizing force for members of the NYVRM. The initial thrust of their efforts was merely to get new voters to the polls, focusing less (if at all) on what voters did after they were activated. We will examine the makeup and behavior of members of Generations X and Y in the following section. For now, it's enough to note that both generations possesss the power to shape America's political landscape because of their size and economic influence. Many NYVRM members were aware of this dormant power and sought to harness the energy for a range of rarely discussed ends.

The NYVRM came about during a time of great technological change and as a result, relied upon emerging media to communicate with potential young voters and share information about candidates and the process. They also relied upon celebrities and star power to entice young people into the electoral process.

The genesis for the NYVRM can be traced to one industry and the organization it created. In the late 1980s, the recording industry came under attack from parent organizations and, ultimately, Congress for producing and selling "indecent material" to America's youth. The rap group "2 Live Crew" was the focal point of the debate and legal wrangling as it was prosecuted under existing obscenity laws for allegedly incendiary and misogynistic lyrics. The political debates expanded, and Congress threatened to mandate obscenity labeling on the packages of cassettes and CDs (a law that ultimately passed) so parents would know what was safe for their children to purchase and play.

Fearing catastrophic impacts on the sale of music, the recording industry united, to fight back. Their main weapon was the growing consumer base among America's youth. However, this sleeping giant of civic activity hadn't been engaged significantly in the political process since the debates of Vietnam and the fight for the right to vote, which was won in 1972. During the 1988 presidential election, for instance, nearly two-thirds of 18- to 24-year-olds remained on the electoral sidelines.

The recording industry knew that any sustained fight against Congress and the courts would require a greater percentage of young people engaged in the electoral and civic processes. Members of Congress had significant incentive for siding with the decency police — the parents of young people who wanted safer musical consumer products were vocal and consistently voted. And their children did not.

The recording industry is a powerful special interest today. But at the time, the "labels" held limited sway in the halls of Congress. And elected officials knew that the industry sought to produce merchandise with few restrictions on what was sold and to whom. Young people were the other variable in the equation. As consumers, they wanted little oversight on what type of music they purchased. But this group rarely paid attention to the electoral process, which made it easy for elected officials to vote for a labeling system. This is another case of legislation happening *to* a segment of Americans, instead of *with* them.

In 1990, Warner Brothers and Capitol Records provided the initial funding and muscle to launch Rock the Vote, a nonprofit, nonpartisan organization whose mission was/is to "engage youth in the political process by incorporating the entertainment community and youth culture into its activities. From actors to musicians, comedians to athletes, Rock the Vote harnesses cutting-edge trends and pop culture to make political participation cool." As part of its branding, Rock the Vote claims to have been founded "in response to a wave of attacks on freedom of speech and artistic expression."

In the eyes of Rock the Vote and its founders, increased registration and voting among America's youth would lead to a shift in the political power base in Washington, D.C., and around the country. Engaging young people in the electoral process would make their voices heard on a range of issues. The organization ultimately sought to quell youth disengagement by making the process "cool." While not the first of its kind, Rock the Vote was a high profile undertaking that led to numerous copycats focused on a specific niche within the 18- to 24-year-old demographic. And it was this specialization that required unprecedented coordination among disparate organizations.

At its inception, Rock the Vote's main activity was registering young people to vote. It created celebrity-based packaging to entice young people to participate and was not really focused on building a bridge to regular, ongoing civic engagement after elections. This has changed slightly over time, particularly as the organization expanded its collaboration with organizations like MTV and their Choose or Lose campaign, which is examined in the following section.

Early on, Rock the Vote recruited celebrities — predominantly musicians — to preach the relative "coolness" of becoming involved in the civic process, via public service announcements (PSAs) and other direct media outreach. The organization hoped that slick ad campaigns filled with "A-list" celebrities would be enough to excite young people, arousing their interest in participation.

Over time, Rock the Vote added a number of activities to its roster, seeking to expand its influence over young people and sustain their interest for elections. A cornerstone of this activity was the creation of street teams, which were squads of young people armed with Rock the Vote merchandise. They attended concerts, school functions and other youth-filled events in an attempt to preach the gospel of civic participation and ultimately, to register young people to vote. More recently, the street teams also provided election guides and other information intended to educate voters.

The recording industry had utilized street teams for years as a marketing tool to sell and promote their products. This personal outreach reinforces the importance of getting involved and builds a measure of accountability for young people who agree to participate. These days, Rock the Vote also coordinates voter registration drives, delivers election information through voter guides and increases interest with get-out-the-vote events.

The following organizational history provides insight into Rock the Vote's evolution and impact on youth voter turnout.

Rock the Vote: Organizational History

Rock the Vote launched its first national ad campaign, "Censorship is Un-American," in 1990, with a string of PSAs featuring celebrities like Iggy Pop, the Red Hot Chili Peppers and Woody Harrelson. The next year, the organization actively supported passage of the Motor Voter Bill, which as outlined earlier, made registering to vote easier for American citizens. Rock the Vote again used artist PSAs, but added a "Dear Senator" postcard campaign. Young people could clip and mail a "Dear Senator" letter that was included in the cardboard CD packages. Rock the Vote's efforts helped with passage of the bill, which was initially vetoed by President Bush (No. 41), but was later signed into law by President Clinton in 1993.

Rock the Vote spent its first two years building a grassroots base of support and worked out the kinks in its PSA campaign and other tactics before totally jumping into the political campaign process. The 1992 presidential election was the first major test of Rock the Vote's new power base. Another series of PSAs was created for this election, featuring artists like R.E.M., En Vogue, Aerosmith, Queen Latifah, Eddie Vedder and Dave Mustaine of metal legend, Megadeth. The PSAs aired on MTV, VH-1, BET and the fledgling FOX network.

Rock the Vote also partnered with the National Association of Secretaries of State to produce PSAs for "Register and Rock the Vote Month." The PSAs were to be aired locally in an attempt to expand the group's reach and influence, while encouraging young people to register. The "Rock the Vote Month" campaign also included an hour-long television special aired on FOX that was filled with musical performances and celebrities who shared important registration information and offered rationales for getting involved. The show was hosted by rapper Queen Latifah and featured appearances by Michael Douglas, Madonna, Tom Cruise, Whoopie Goldberg, etc. Rock the Vote and its partners registered more than 350,000 young Americans for the 1992 elections, which helped produce the highest youth turnout for a presidential election since 1972. The impact of Rock the Vote and other NYVRM organizations will be examined in subsequent chapters. For now, we will simply evaluate their histories to produce a timeline for the NYVRM.

In 1993, President Bill Clinton praised Rock the Vote for its role in helping to pass the Motor Voter legislation during the White House bill-signing ceremony. They built upon this legislative victory by lobbying for passage of the National and Community Service Trust Act, which was intended to spur volunteerism among young people. The bill ultimately passed and was signed into law by President Clinton on September 21, 1993.

Rock the Vote next turned its attention to the 1994 midterm elections, where they moved beyond merely registering people to vote through PSAs and ad campaigns. Instead, they sought to influence the elections by arming young people with detailed information about issues. They created and passed out more than a million brochures entitled "Rock the System: A Guide to Health Care for Young Americans." This brochure provided detailed information on health care issues that were important to young people at the time.

Rock the Vote geared up for the 1996 elections by launching a slew of new programs. Again, most of these efforts were geared toward registering and educating voters, without pointing them in a direction for action. The first new program was an unprecedented attempt to use the telephone to register voters. The organization launched 1-800-REGISTER, which became 1-800-ROCK VOTE as the election neared. Interested young people could call and receive the phone number for election offices in order to locate polling places, request absentee ballots or obtain other important election information.

The 1-800-REGISTER campaign included displays in more than 8,000 record stores nationwide. A flyer at each display provided the hotline number and other important election information. Participants who used the phone number also received a reminder card in the mail a week before the election, intended to reinforce their commitment to vote. MCI was a significant underwriter of the 1996 campaign, which in addition to the hotline included the first Web site with online voter registration capabilities. They called the World Wide Web campaign NetVote '96. It was also during the 1996 elections that Rock the Vote cemented an expansive partnership with MTV. The two organizations registered nearly 40,000 voters through this phone campaign alone.

All told, in 1996 Rock the Vote and its partners registered more than 500,000 new voters through radio partnerships, concert tours, MTV Choose or Lose bus, the 1-800-REGISTER campaign and NetVote '96. Rock the Vote also launched its "Radio Rocks the Vote" campaign in 1996 and, in collaboration with MTV, published 200,000 copies of a free non-partisan voter guide. The document outlined candidate positions on a range of issues prominently on the radar of young people at the time.

Rock the Vote's motives changed a bit in 1997, as it launched an aggressive grassroots issue campaign, which attempted to beat back what it saw as anti-First Amendment legislation popping up around the nation. The organization built a national network of volunteers who worked in a local, grassroots fashion to provide young people with information on the issue in hopes of getting them to engage in debates in the halls of government at all levels of the American political system. This effort was the culmination of what Rock the Vote's founders envisioned when they created the group nearly a decade before.

Rock the Vote underwent its biggest change in 1998, with a massive reorganization that altered the group's focus and structure. The new mission statement read "[Rock the Vote is] dedicating itself to protecting freedom of expression, and helping young people realize and utilize their power to affect change in the civic and political lives of their communities." They again partnered with MCI and joined up with the American Association of Retired People (AARP) to launch "Rock the Vote 'Rocks the Ages' with NetVote '98." This Website built upon the foundation of their first "net" effort by including election information and voter registration capabilities for Americans of all ages, in all locations. The organization also launched "Rock the Vote Every Day," a public education campaign focused more on the long-term civic engagement of young people, not just voter turnout. Combined, Rock the Vote and its partners registered more than 250,000 new voters for the 1998 midterm elections.

In 1999, Rock the Vote embraced a new tactic: peer-to-peer influencing. Young people told their stories of community service as a method for inspiring peer civic activity beyond Election Day. Again, PSAs were at the heart of this initiative, and they appeared on Fox, ABC, MTV and TBS. The Rock the Vote Every Day campaign also expanded to include "Use Your Power to Rock the Vote Every Day," a toolkit for political activism. It was distributed through record stores, community organizations and schools across the nation.

As with all previous major elections, Rock the Vote reinvented itself in 2000, updating the technology at its disposal and adding new arrows to its collective quiver. This time they modernized their Website (www.rockthevote.com) and updated the online voter registration application. This tool alone accounted for an additional 165,000 newly registered voters. In addition, 20,000 visitors to the site applied for absentee ballots. Rock the Vote also embarked on a 25-city, four-month bus tour intended to provide young people across the country with information and voter registration tools. A cadre of musicians, actors and other celebrities joined them at stops along the way. Participants included the cast of NBC's "The West Wing," Outkast, Hootie & the Blowfish and many more.

Like its longtime supporter Madonna, the campaign got a little more controversial after each reincarnation. A shocking new string of print PSAs was launched that told young voters to "Piss off a Politician" and vote. The spots were placed in national magazines like *Rolling Stone, Vibe, Young and Modern* and *The Source*. They also continued their outreach to diverse segments of the youth voting population. The 2000 effort included "Rap the Vote 2000," a partnership with Russell Simmons' "360HipHop" that asked members of the hip hop community to set an example for young people by living up to the mantra: "Register. Vote. Represent." Television PSAs featured appearances by Puff Daddy (ne, P. Diddy), Rosie Perez and L.L. Cool J.

New partnerships served to expand the organization's reach. Rock the Vote partnered with the Southwest Voter Participation Project to develop TV PSAs targeted to young Latinos, encouraging them to register and vote. The spots appeared primarily on MTV. A partnership was also created with the Gay & Lesbian Alliance Against Defamation that produced a series of print public service announcements targeting the gay and lesbian community. By the close of Election 2000, Rock the Vote and its partners had registered more than 500,000 new voters.

In 2001, Rock the Vote expanded its grassroots outreach by launching 15 new Community Street Teams across the country. According to Rock the Vote, more than 120 young people volunteered for the program and contributed more than 3,000 volunteer hours through 242 field activities that resulted in the following: the collection of 31,565 signatures for a hate crime petition; the distribution of 79,000 "Fight For Your Rights: Take a Stand Against Discrimination" guides; and the registration of 4,000 young voters.

The grassroots approach was enhanced by a partnership with MTV on the network's "Fight for Your Rights: Take a Stand Against Discrimination" campaign. Rock the Vote built the ground troops for the campaign and created "Community Invasion" events around the Total Request Live show's tour, which played in front of thousands of high school students.

Rock the Vote launched its most ambitious programs during the 2002 midterm elections. The first step was an expanded Rock the Vote Street Team effort in 35 cities, recruiting more than 1,200 volunteers who contributed greater than 8,200 hours of volunteer service at hundreds of community festivals, concerts, parades and other local events. At this point, the organization grew in stature. Now formerly-prominent civic organizations hitched their stars to Rock the Vote's campaigns in the hopes of repositioning themselves and finding new members and participants. For instance, the NAACP partnered with Rock the Vote and Russell Simmons/Def Jam Records to expand the "Rap the Vote" campaign. The resulting partnership managed education and registration initiatives during a nationwide fall tour.

Rock the Vote's 2002 efforts also included:

- Supplying more than 150 American community organizations and schools with free voter registration kits, Rock the Vote paraphernalia and Rock the Vote Every Day resource guides.
- Partnering with 85 radio stations to air Rock and Rap the Vote PSAs and "Get Out the Vote" messages by artists such as Eve, Chris Rock, Puddle of Mudd and Kelly Osbourne.
- Reaching millions of young people online with voter registration and mobilization flash pieces. The new online strategy also included Web banners with seven site partners that led to more than one million impressions.
- A 34-city national voter registration bus tour sponsored by 7UP included a "Rock the Vote Soap Box," giving young people the chance to share their views on issues.
- Serving as the voter registration partner for more than 20 concert tours.

Finally, in February 2002, Rock the Vote took another ambitious step in their efforts to directly intervene in the lives of young people. They hosted the 9/11 Youth Summit, which was a two-day meeting attended by 50 youth leaders from across the country who discussed their reactions to the events of September 11, 2001. This summit included a dialogue between youth leaders, policy experts and government officials. Information from the event was synthesized into a report that Rock the Vote delivered to every member of Congress in an attempt to highlight the concerns of America's youth.

Rock the Vote sought new partners and updated their technologies in advance of the 2004 presidential elections. Ben & Jerry's ice cream became a supporter of the voter registration campaign, who's website was overhauled to simplify the registration process, while creating "cool incentives" for young people to get involved. And they continued to expand the Rock the Vote Community Street Team program.

In its more than 15-year history, Rock the Vote has recruited thousands of volunteers and launched hundreds of PSAs and other media efforts to excite young people about the electoral process and ultimately, register them to vote. Over time, their programs became more robust and evolved to focus on building bridges to long-term civic participation, instead of just getting people registered and to the polls. Rock the Vote has been very successful at its cornerstone endeavor: registering young people to vote. To date, Rock the Vote has successfully added nearly 2,000,000 young people to America's voter rolls. These numbers are impressive, but the overall impact of Rock the Vote's activity will be debated in a section about the "Next Greatest Generation," following an examination of MTV's efforts.

Chapter 16

MTV "Choose or Lose" and Efforts to Increase Youth Voter Participation

Much of Rock the Vote's early work was made possible by its close affiliation with MTV. This cable channel that began playing only music videos in 1983 has evolved into a global pop culture empire whose influence extends into multiple elements of American life. It is the epicenter of teen attitudes, fashion and language, and not only reflects what's trendy and what's hip, but it also determines it. In addition to music videos (which appear less and less frequently these days), the network offers a variety of programming that includes entertainment news, sports shows and reality television. In fact, many experts credit the network with launching the American reality TV genre in the early 1990s when "The Real World" first aired.

About that same time, MTV began a partnership with Rock the Vote and the organization's efforts to increase youth political and civic education and activity. Over time, its money, power and reach have made MTV one of the most prominent members of the National Youth Voter Registration Movement. From its inception, MTV's political activity was richer and more robust than that of Rock the Vote (which was founded by the recording industry well-in-advance of MTV's own programming) and other NYVRM members.

The network used its increasingly powerful news department and "Choose or Lose" campaign to promote the goals of the movement. And in the process it assisted other start-up campaigns like Rock the Vote, to gain name ID and build support through the celebrity community. Partnering with MTV gave these new NYVRM organizations street credibility and traction among youth. Strategically speaking, MTV had a two-pronged attack that differed from its partners: utilize the airwaves to educate young voters about the importance of civic participation, the issues and candidate positions; and register people to vote. The latter goal was accomplished through these partnerships with, and economic support of other NYVRM organizations.

MTV partnered with Rock the Vote to create much of its programming during the network's first foray into civic education and mobilization. As outlined last chapter, the majority of MTV's interaction with Rock the Vote and other NYVRM members was in the form of financial support and co-branding of activities. The support included providing free airtime for Rock the Vote PSAs and other announcements, hosting local grassroots programs and registering young people to vote at concerts, malls and sporting events.

MTV began to craft its own civic identity by launching its "Choose or Lose" program in 1992. According to the network, this program is a "comprehensive pro-social campaign to inform young adults about the political process, voice their most urgent political concerns, compel leading presidential candidates to address those concerns, and mobilize massive numbers of young adults aged 18 to 30, to register and vote." The program launched during the 1992 New Hampshire primary with candidate interviews and limited coverage of results. Candidates were apprehensive at first about dealing with the youth-oriented network and its "news" department. But ultimately, MTV's ratings and target audience were too compelling to resist, which helped the network gain candidate interviews and information that Rock the Vote and other NYVRM organizations could not. By agreeing to interviews, the candidates received free "adbites" — slick news spots created when portions of the interviews appeared repeatedly in MTV news segments and other programming.

MTV eventually garnered a level of credibility with candidates through its efforts to collect political information used for educating young people and getting them to vote. This proved invaluable as the civic programming expanded, requiring greater candidate access. The success of MTV's New Hampshire news coverage allowed the network to move into its next phase in the 1992 program, candidate town halls: "Choose or Lose" campaign segments and other programming intended to provide detailed election information to young viewers.

As mentioned in the introduction to this book, the 1992 elections were my first, and I remember MTV's efforts vividly. Their involvement added considerable excitement to the contest because of the network's ability to place issues and candidates into the context of current youth experience. This is most evidenced by a Ford Motor Company-sponsored town hall featuring then candidate Bill Clinton. This 90-minute special, viewed by nearly 780,000 people in its live airing, consisted of a question and answer session between the candidate and nearly 200 audience members. The forum provided members of Generation X with the kind of candidate access that really hadn't existed before.

The questions were direct, as were Bill Clinton's answers. And it seemed as if nothing was off limits. In fact, in one of my generation's least impressive moments, an audience member asked Bill Clinton if he wore boxers or briefs. This is also the venue where Clinton made the memorable gaffe of admitting to trying marijuana, but claiming he had never inhaled. The audience may not have believed the answer, but nonetheless, they were overwhelmingly moved by the unprecedented access to the candidate and his charisma and intelligence.

Interviews also took place with vice presidential candidate Al Gore and a reluctant President George Bush. This trend continued in 1996 as MTV news anchor Tabitha Soren interviewed several candidates, including Bob Dole, Phil Gramm, Lamar Alexander, Steve Forbes and Pat Buchanan. MTV followed candidates along the campaign trail and held interviews on the network's latest creation, a 45-foot Choose or Lose Bus, which traveled to campuses, malls, concerts and other venues across America.

Reporters, musicians and organizational partners, like Rock the Vote, would set up registration tables and a stage at each stop along the way to entice young people to get involved. An array of marketing techniques were used to get the attention of young people, including TV screens playing the latest music videos, free giveaways and live performances by popular artists. This grassroots approach allowed the network to take the information directly to potential young voters. This time around, young people were asked to fill out pledge cards that "committed them" to go to the polls on Election Day and "Rock the Vote."

The featured bands would also add commentary during their performances — although not often substantive — about the elections and why being involved was, in essence, cool. MTV also expanded its programming to include "Choose or Lose Reports" in 1996. This again cemented their role in the NYVRM as being more than a flashy campaign to increase publicity for the network. These programs provided candidate, issue and election information in the form of 30-second to four-minute segments woven into each day's newscast. Snippets of interviews with candidates, celebrities and potential voters were usually intended to entice viewers into watching upcoming programs that examined issues like AIDS, domestic violence and the environment in greater detail. Issues of the day were portrayed in a light that made them real for young people, informing potential Generation X voters about why being involved mattered.

Finally, MTV published a 45-page voter manual that was distributed at each stop of the bus tour, at concerts and online. The book highlighted the biographies and positions of candidates in various statewide and national races across the country. When combined with Rock the Vote's efforts, the 1996 education activities were the most robust to date of any NYVRM entity.

MTV was much less visible during the 2000 elections, perhaps because youth voter turnout dropped in the 1996 elections in spite of the network's extensive mobilization efforts and financial expenditures. Media executives often say that the reason they don't cover politics in more detail during the news or devote more time to elections is because people do not demand it. Perhaps MTV felt that their viewers expressed a powerful disinterest at the polls in 1996, which predicted diminished voter participation in 2000 — a lesson they heeded, which resulted in little political activity for MTV during one of the closest elections in American history.

However, 9/11 seemed to change the network's focus, as it did with most elements of American daily life. The network seemed to find a new civic purpose, and began airing programming about the conflict in Iraq, religion, race and sexuality. MTV's renewed vigor for issues and politics culminated with a significantly more visible Choose or Lose campaign for the 2004 elections.

The network set a bold goal of mobilizing more than 20 million young adults in their target demographic — 18 to 30 years of age — and bringing them to the polls. Called "20 Million Loud," the campaign carried on the network's role in the NYVRM of providing detailed election information and the goal of inspiring people to action.

This campaign had a strong peer-to-peer component, the impact of which will be discussed in later chapters of this section.

MTV also continued to coordinate and cultivate a diverse coalition of NYVRM partners, including Rock the Vote, Hip-Hop Team Vote, World Wrestling Entertainment's "Smackdown Your Vote!," New Voters Project, Declare Yourself, and nearly 100 other grassroots groups that comprise the Youth Vote Coalition. As always, the NYVRM's activities were visible online, on-air and in-person. The program got underway in January 2004 with the first of two MTV News specials, "Diary: Gideon in Iraq." The second program, "Louder Now," aired on February 2.

MTV's activities culminated in October with a new program that had not been attempted before by NYVRM organizations. This "PRE-Lection" allowed young voters to cast ballots for their preferred presidential candidate online and via text messaging. According to MTV and MTV2 President, Van Toffler, "The goal of 'Choose or Lose 2004' and '20 Million Loud' is to give this enormous pool of potential voters the tools they need to make informed choices, get involved in the political process, and become motivated to make the ultimate choice in our democracy."

The world changed on September 11, 2001. But America's new role in a global conflict with terrorism wasn't the only explanation for MTV's ambitious goals in 2004. The abysmal participation of 18- to 30-year-olds in Election 2000 also played a significant role. Barely 30 percent of this critical block voted. So MTV revived their efforts and hoped to elevate participation by providing motivation, education and excitement to the campaign season. MTV estimated that in 2004, nearly 20 million votes were up for grabs for candidates in both parties since young adults were equally split between the Democratic and Republican parties in 2000.

The 2004 Choose or Lose campaign included: regular news segments about the candidates and election activity; issue-based specials; candidate interviews; convention coverage and local grassroots events. The local activity was intended to drive awareness, excitement and voter registration. The campaign closed with an election night wrap-up special. In language intended to remind the candidates about MTV's previous sway with voters in 1992 and other elections, the network announced that, "it is ultimately up to the politicians and political parties to appeal to this powerful bloc," a challenge to engage young people on their turf — or at least on the airwaves of this youth-directed network.

Perhaps most noteworthy was MTV's ambitious effort to get people to the polls — the network's polls. MTV held an exclusive "PRE-Lection" at www.mtv.com in October 2004, which was only open to young people who were registered to vote in their home state for the real presidential contest. This was a great tool for getting young Americans registered. This non-binding online faux election was intended to raise excitement and traffic at MTV's Web site. Once there, potential voters found the resources to ensure they were registered in time for the November contest. John Kerry won the groundbreaking election in a landslide, garnering more than 61 percent of the vote (59,660) compared to President Bush's 35 percent (38,025).

MTV followed former Democratic presidential candidate Howard Dean's lead by relying heavily on MeetUp.com's tools for driving its local outreach campaign. Again in conjunction with Rock the Vote, MTV and MeetUp.com held local gatherings on the first Tuesday of every month that gave young people a venue for discussing the issues that mattered in their communities. These meetings also allowed them to build local contacts and relationships. Ultimately though, MTV hoped the meetings would be a viral, grassroots mechanism for adding educated young people to voter rolls in 2004.

MTV relied on the support of numerous partners to ensure success for the 2004 version of its Choose or Lose campaign. Rock the Vote was the engine for online and primary grassroots voter registration efforts. Other partners included Project Vote Smart, National Council of La Raza, Black Youth Vote, the New Voters Project, CIRCLE Research, the NAACP, Harvard University Institute of Politics and other organizations across the political, racial and issue spectrums. Cingular Wireless was the program's primary sponsor, helping voters to participate in the PRE-Lection online and via their wireless devices.

MTV's civic efforts have grown more robust over time, providing the engine for NYVRM activities. The network served as the umbrella for information and relationships in the NYVRM because of their access to young people *and* capital. The 2004 elections signaled the pinnacle of their growth and influence, as MTV became a full-service education tool. Their efforts allowed people to learn about the issues and candidates, while registering them to vote and building enthusiasm for voting with unique activities like the PRE-Lection.

Chapter 17

Results: How Did the NYVRM Members Fare?

Analyzing the results from three election cycles in the 1990s proves a lot about the success and failures of the National Youth Voter Registration Movement. Each organization experienced a number of programmatic successes. Unfortunately, it's clear these efforts failed to bring about long-term, widespread civic engagement among their young target audience. The lessons gleaned from these experiences provide important insight into what effectively increases participation levels and what doesn't. And understanding these failings will help current and future organizations engage young people in the civic process.

The 1992 presidential election garnered the largest youth voter turnout since 1972. Nearly 48 percent of 18- to 20-year-olds registered to vote and 38.5 percent actually went to the polls. In the next age bracket, 21- to 24-year-olds, 55 percent registered to vote and almost 46 percent pulled a lever.

These numbers were better than the 1988 election registration and turnout totals. For that contest between Michael Dukakis and President Ronald Reagan, slightly less than 44 percent of 18- to 20-year-olds registered, and only 33 percent went to the polls. A little more than 50 percent of 21- to 24-year-olds were registered and roughly 38 percent went to the polls. That meant that voter activity in both age brackets was up nearly 5 percent in 1992.

A number of reasons account for the 1992 voting increase. The first and potentially most significant reason was the candidates on the top of the ballot. Both Bill Clinton and H. Ross Perot had mass youth appeal, while President George Bush seemed stiff and disinterested in young people, their issues and their votes.

It was clear that Bill Clinton sensed the power of the sleeping youth vote, which probably explains why he appeared on more hip and daring TV programming than any presidential candidate before him. Candidate Clinton appeared in the landmark MTV town hall meeting discussed in the previous chapter and spoke with Phil Donahue, Larry King and late night host Arsenio Hall. Clinton even went so far as to don a pair of Ray Ban™ sunglasses and play saxophone with Arsenio's band.

But thankfully, there is a more substantive issue to explain the rise in youth voter interest and participation. Bill Clinton placed significant attention on youth-centered issues. His ideas and policy proposals resonated with members of Generation X in a manner unlike any other candidate since John F. Kennedy. The election probably would have turned out differently if Clinton was all sizzle and no substance. In other words, young people appreciated his appearances on hip shows and his fashion savvy (a relative term by today's standards obviously). But they would have tuned out if he had ignored substantive discussions of issues. Clinton did manage to appeal to the youth style and intellect. But he also focused policy recommendations and speeches on issues like: universal healthcare; making college loans more available and affordable; and improving and preserving the world's physical environment.

As a result, many of the young voters who went to the polls in 1992 felt that Bill Clinton was sincerely interested in their issues and their votes. More accurately, many young voters went to the polls because Bill Clinton focused on their hopes, dreams and needs. As outlined in this book's introduction, Generation X held Clinton in the same high regard as our parents viewed John Kennedy. Many in 1992 believed they had a chance to be involved in a modern renaissance of service and government that would reshape the world. It can't be understated: Clinton made a generation believe that they had a voice. And more importantly, that they could take action to solve the challenges facing our flattening world. The parallels to President Kennedy were most visible in Clinton's focus on local, national and international service. Clinton hoped to make the world a better place by directly engaging young people in the trenches.

The candidacy of H. Ross Perot also played a significant role in election turnout and the overall results. Perot garnered 22 percent of all first time and 18- to 24-year-old voters. Much of Perot's appeal revolved around his specially cultivated "outsider" status. He was a political neophyte who had spent years building a successful business empire. And to the appreciation of many young people, he was not a politician who toiled inside the political beltway. Members of Generation X had grown tired of political gridlock driven by the two-party system. Some young people perceived Perot's candidacy as a viable alternative to the mainstream and an opportunity to shake things up politically. In Perot, many disaffected youth saw a chance to send a message to members of Congress, changing the power structure forever and cementing their seat at the table. Howard Dean seemed to offer a similar alternative during the early stages of the 2004 election.

Perot bought time on network television during prime viewing hours. While Clinton was hitting the talk show circuit, Perot was hosting a series of infomercials. The programs were an opportunity for him to highlight the challenges facing modern American society. The airtime also gave him the chance to discuss the need for tax breaks and rail against the gridlock often created by our two-party political system.

Perot offered few, if any, truly substantive policy recommendations, but his message was different from that of previous presidential candidates and refreshing to many people who were tiring of partisan platforms and political platitudes. Most notable was his business management approach to tackling America's flagging economy (which was, in reality, coming out of recession). This novel approach stirred enough passion to affect the election's outcome.

Perot was a true force, gaining key swing voter support while also stealing a meaningful percentage of core members of both the Democratic and Republican parties. More Republicans jumped ship than Democrats due to Perot's conservative fiscal rhetoric that emphasized tax cuts and better budget management. It's this siphoning of votes from the Republican Party that played a deciding factor in Clinton's razor-thin victory in 1992.

Some credit does need to be extended to Rock the Vote, MTV and other NYVRM members for President Clinton's victory. Their emphasis on voter registration and education diminished two key barriers to youth participation. Rock the Vote and its partners registered more than 350,000 young people and claim to have mobilized nearly two million voters from their inception to 2003. However, as we will see from the election data, registering large pockets of voters is important, but it isn't enough to ensure consistent voter turnout and long-term civic engagement.

The 1994 and 1996 elections raise questions about whether the NYVRM is effective at much more than voter registration. Voter turnout in 1994 dropped from 1992 levels. Only 16 percent of 18- to 20-year-olds went to the polls and 22 percent of 21- to 24-year-olds participated. That was a two percent drop from 1990 — the last non-presidential election — among 18- to 20-year-olds. And voter participation among 21- to 24-year-old voters remained constant from 1990.

It might not seem significant at first glance that 18- to 20-year-old participation dropped two points or that 21- to 24-year-olds were static at 22 percent. But consider these numbers more closely for a moment. Youth voter turnout in 1992 was at its highest level in 24 years and it was also the most political enthusiasm in a generation. Voter registration continued to increase through the efforts of NYVRM organizations in the years following that election. But — and here is the important fact — registrants didn't turn out to the polls. So why wasn't the same enthusiasm palpable? Why didn't turnout continue to surge in later elections? Why didn't it continue at a fever pitch rather than sink to previously low levels?

As previously outlined, Bill Clinton's success was due in part, to the power of the youth vote and NYVRM mobilization and education efforts. He promised a new America in 1992, and voters — particularly the young and optimistic — expected immediate results. Clinton struggled early in his first term to make progress with the existing Washington political and power structure, and he failed to deliver on many of his campaign promises. In short, the Clinton Administration failed to deliver the goods early on.

Issues from the campaign received some attention (gays in the military, universal health care proposals, etc.) at the start of his administration, but didn't result in legislative victories. Clinton battled with Congress and lost, failing to produce the Camelot that so many had hoped and dreamed about. And some early missteps like the failed raid on the Branch Davidian compound in Waco, Texas, and an unwillingness to battle through the proposed ban on gays in the military made Clinton look lost. Many voters came to view him as a weak leader, even those who two years before were ardent fans and supporters.

These failures and modest legislative results took place in an increasingly partisan and negative Washington cauldron. The "Contract with America," driven by conservative Speaker of the House Newt Gingrich, produced an ideological stalemate that was negatively charged. The partisan gridlock and Clinton's lackluster performance combined to turn-off hordes of young voters (and older voters as well). Many felt betrayed and powerless against special interests and partisan forces. Interestingly, this forced many voters to turn away from politics and look for local solutions through volunteerism and professional pursuits.

This is the first lesson gleaned from the actions of NYVRM organizations: Registration and education are important. However, Rock the Vote, MTV and others, focused strictly on voter mobilization. Few, if any of their programs, focused on building long-term civic participation. As a result, these new and young voters became civic and political bystanders again, once the election and marketing bonanza concluded.

While thousands of young people heeded President Clinton's call to service, agreeing to volunteer in AmeriCorps, Vista, City Year and other initiatives, they failed to engage politicians directly. They didn't call en masse to voice opinions about the issues outlined above. On average, Generation X sat silently on the governmental sidelines as legislation happened to them.

To be truly successful, organizations (whether in the NYVRM or not) need to develop programming that builds interest in the civic process so that people stay connected and involved long

after an election. This requires instilling civic passion and a desire to remain engaged for the long-term, while providing tools to success-fully navigate the political process. The lack of participation from this new reservoir of young voters created in 1992 meant their issues either dropped off the collective Congressional radar or failed to pass on the floor of the House and Senate.

The 1996 election provided the NYVRM a chance for redemption. Organizations geared up for a more robust undertaking in this elec-tion cycle. And they were buoyed by the fact that President Clinton became a force in Washington after the initial legislative blunders, battling Newt Gingrich and advancing his own political agenda. His charisma — on full display throughout the campaign — ultimately helped the president build a track record of success on the policy front. America's economy was growing rapidly with the first stages of the "dot-com" boom taking shape, leading members of Generation X to successful and meaningful employment following college.

These factors created a positive environment and a great deal of potential for the NYVRM organizations to succeed in elevating voter turnout in 1996. Unfortunately, this success failed to materialize. The 18- to 24-year-old voter turnout in 1996 was the lowest of any presi-dential election in history! That's right, in history. Only 31 percent of eligible 18- to 20-year-olds went to the polls, *a 7 percent drop* from 1992. And a little more than 33 percent of 21- to 24-year-olds both-ered to cast a ballot, which was *a 12 percent decline* from 1992.

How is that possible? Rock the Vote single-handedly registered more than 515,000 Generation X voters that election. And as outlined above, all the indicators pointed to voter enthusiasm and greater turn-out. First, the numbers reinforce one of the major themes of this book: Voter registration alone is not enough to get people to the polls and then remain involved in the civic process after Election Day. While the past 10 to 12 years only provide three presidential elections and a handful of congressional campaigns to judge from, indicators suggest that registration alone isn't the answer.

The outcome of the 1996 election was obvious early on, which was certainly a factor in the diminished youth turnout. Early polling and media coverage made it clear from the start that Senator Bob Dole would provide a weak challenge to President Clinton. This removed the incentive for many people to go out and fight for their candidate. The election seemed virtually over before it had a chance to heat up.

Perhaps more importantly, the candidates' agendas were much different in 1996 than in 1992. In that campaign, candidates made significant attempts to engage young people. Generation X's issues were discussed, and candidates met young people on their turf. In a complete reversal, both President Clinton and Senator Dole all but ignored young voters and their issues in 1996.

President Clinton's outreach to the NYVRM included one stop on the MTV Choose or Lose tour. He all but abandoned the successful 1992 youth strategy that was an important factor in his victory. Clinton also avoided the talk show circuit this time around, perhaps out of fear that he would have to answer tough questions on Whitewater and the failed universal health care initiative driven by First Lady Hillary Clinton. Regardless of the reason, President Clinton played it safe by staying away from Generation X venues and focused on a more mainstream policy agenda that appealed to older Americans.

For his part, Senator Dole seemed frightened of engaging young people. MTV provided easy access to a large number of youth voters even though it wasn't the only conduit available. Yet Dole only took advantage of one interview opportunity with the network. Turns out this choice was probably the correct one as he was visibly uncomfortable with the format, the audience and the line of questioning, not to mention that he seemingly had little interest in or connection to the issues facing Generation X.

MTV's efforts were more robust in 1996, and Rock the Vote continued registering young people in large numbers. Yet these efforts failed to move the youth participation needle. Young people were still smarting from the particularly negative tone established in Washington during the mid-1990s. And both candidates left them feeling alienated or marginalized in the process. These factors combined to leave young voters — even the newly registered — on the political sidelines.

Taken as a whole, the NYVRM experienced a number of successes. From registering nearly two million voters in less than 10 years to developing innovative programming that educated young people about the candidates, the process and the need for being involved. But missing from these NYVRM initiatives was the grassroots, personal element that makes the civic process meaningful for people. It is the peer-to-peer contact that helps young people overcome the dual barriers of the perception of powerlessness and disdain for the system.

While their program scope and effectiveness in registering young people is impressive, members of the NYVRM failed to bring about the political power base its founders had hoped for and predicted. Their efforts were supposed to lead to more than just significantly increased voter registration and turnout. Again, the NYVRM had its roots in the music industry's efforts to build an enormous army of *engaged* young people who would turn back "harmful and intrusive" legislative efforts like "Parental Advisory" labels on music, movies and other media.

Additional factors outlined previously, led the NYVRM efforts to miss their mark. The initial efforts of Rock the Vote and other organizations relied upon star power to gain visibility and to increase involvement. The PSA approach, for which Michael Stipe, Madonna and LL Cool J preached the importance of "Rocking the Vote," failed to connect people to policy and the process. These campaigns were all sizzle and no substance. And in at least one instance, the campaign backfired because it became known that Madonna wasn't even a regular voter. The PSA strategy was a great way to grab attention for a fledgling organization. It certainly added an entertainment value and celebrity cache which increased initial interest in the program. Yet, there was no in-depth, substantive program, which would have truly cemented the importance of being involved.

Additionally, the NYVRM's initial efforts were driven almost exclusively by a PSA campaign that talked *to* voters via TV, but not *with them* in a grassroots, peer-to-peer manner. Members of the NYVRM were successful at grabbing the attention of potential young voters for at least a brief period of time. But they didn't use that time effectively. Entertainment was the central tool for enticing people into the process, making it cool to engage and "Rock the Vote on Election Day." But cool doesn't guarantee action.

MTV's Choose or Lose college tour is a prime example of the NYVRM's failings. Students registered to vote and picked up campaign information amidst the glow of music videos and rock stars. One of the program's main accountability measures was getting people to fill in an election reminder card that read, "I will rock the system by exercising my right to vote on November 5, 1996, because ____ _____." The problem is that MTV would pull up the tent and head to another town the next day to recruit more registrants, never personally reconnecting with the people they just encouraged to register and vote. Young people who filled out the cards were accountable to a postcard, not a person.

The following responses were actually written on MTV and other organizations' postcards. And they highlight another problem with the post card approach. Respondents intended to rock the system on Election Day because: "I'm cool," "Bob Dole is an ass," "I have cable," "I'm the smartest man alive," etc. Many people filling out the cards failed to take the process seriously. The importance of voting and being engaged in the civic process was lost in all the celebrity hoopla and free swag.

Many young people who filled out cards or registered to vote in this process didn't learn the true importance of being involved. Nor did they gain a greater connection to the process. For many students along the Rock the Vote and Choose or Lose tours, filling out a pledge card seemed like the cool thing to do. Or it allowed them to meet celebrities and receive free promotional materials like t-shirts, hats, etc. Obviously this isn't true for every young person who filled out a card or engaged in NYVRM activities. **But the lesson is clear. A civic engagement program will only be successful if it is substantive and has personal accountability measures that stand the test of time, distance and celebrity.**

Finally, the lacking sense of civic duty detailed throughout the book is a major obstacle that NYVRM programs failed to overcome on a sustained level. The responsibilities of citizenship are lost concepts to significant segments of our society today. The values and requirements are taught less frequently to our newest and youngest citizens. And so, the NYVRM organizations were unable to overcome the missing civic core values of a generation, even though they made significant investments of money, time and human capital.

We shouldn't write off people — young and old — that do not regularly engage in the civic process. But the NYVRM efforts prove we need to place significant emphasis on America's future — its children. Missing from the NYVRM were programs at the local level that build an understanding of what it means to be involved in the civic process, and why it matters for people currently too young to vote. As stated earlier, teaching civics at an early age and reinforcing those lessons over time is a central element in ensuring long-term participation.

Rock the Vote, MTV and other members of the NYVRM provided young people with the necessary first steps for engaging in the electoral and larger civic process. However, efforts that rely entirely on image and not substance — like using celebrities for PSAs and to promote the organization — fail to hold the attention of young people long enough to instill a sense of civic duty and involvement. P. Diddy and his "Vote or Die" campaign (2004), which will be examined in the next section, is a perfect example of making voting "cool," without making it relevant and meaningful to the individual. And in the end, the effort failed to bring about a significant increase in voter turnout, which was the truest measure of success.

These efforts are particularly weak when not combined with a local, peer-driven approach to building awareness, enthusiasm and long-term engagement. The partnerships created during more than a decade of work provide an opportunity for the NYVRM to succeed in the future, but they must switch focus by adding a grassroots, peer-to-peer approach — particularly with the next generation of voters. Young people already skeptical of the civic process need a substantive reason to engage — not a gimmick. The efforts to date have been meaningful, but they are only small steps on the road of building a more engaged and responsible civic society.

Section V

Chapters 18 – 30

The Greatest Generation That Never Was: Events That Failed To Move America's Youth.

Chapter 18

Introduction

The first section of this book examined general civic participation trends, including a history of America's "Greatest Generation," followed by some clear-cut reasons why civic and electoral participation have declined during the past 30-plus years. The initial chapters detailed the "ideal" for active engagement in American civic life. They provided insight into the mettle that tested a generation and forged the men and woman who grew up with The Great Depression and World War II into pillars of enduring freedom at home and around the world.

But over time, participation waned as people became distrustful of government and many of its actions (or in many cases, the inability of government to advance issues and ideas). However, people didn't only lose faith in the institution of government. They also lost faith in the individuals leading our democratic institutions.

Section two of this book outlined specific barriers to active participation. The information presented in that section explained why the simple phrase "cynicism and apathy," which is so frequently thrown about to explain diminishing participation, is not the entire reason for the decline. It is just one reason why hundreds of thousands, even millions of Americans have turned away from the civic process.

In those sections, we examined the "why." Now we need to complete the picture of "who" is, and is not participating in the civic process. The first chapter examined the ideal for participation. The next will outline the worst-case scenario. This section focuses on "the Greatest Generation that never was" and the series of events that should have inspired it to action. As we'll see, these events left them even more disinterested in the civic process. Political rhetoric, extreme partisanship, a failure of elected officials to advance the youth agenda and a host of other issues will be examined as causes of the failure to increase youth engagement.

Chapter 19

The History of Youth Electoral Participation

Civic participation in varying forms and among all age groups and demographics has declined during the past 30-plus years, leading to some of the lowest activity in American history. The most egregious offenders of civic inactivity are America's youth — those 18 to 30 years of age. Young Americans vote less, volunteer less and, in general, pay less attention to the world and issues around them than any other generation in history. In this chapter we'll look at rates of electoral participation among young people, while outlining some of the basic reasons for their disinterest and disengagement.

I speak frequently at Rotary Clubs, community groups and conferences that examine issues of civic participation. Quite often, the simple statement that America's youth are not engaged in the civic process is met with a shrug and that age-old phrase "kids will be kids." It's as if people, through their disinterest in the notion, are saying that they too were dispassionate about politics or world issues in their youth, and that this is to be expected and accepted. People share with me that they became more involved as they joined the workforce, purchased a home, or encountered government in other, more personal ways. And that they believe today's youth will follow the same pattern of engagement.

While statistically and historically accurate, these people are missing a more important point — that America's youth are less involved than previous generations of young people. Whether we're talking about civic knowledge or action, today's youth are less interested, informed and less involved than any generation of young people in American history. According to an October 29, 2003 CNN/USA Today/Gallup Poll, only 69 percent of young people claim to follow politics, which is in stark contrast to the 81 percent of Americans 29 years of age, or older. The survey also found that young people are three times less likely to be engaged on issues and current events than older Americans.

Young people are less involved in the electoral process as well. Voter participation among 18- to 24-year-olds has decreased by almost 20 percent since 1972 when 18-year-olds were given the right to vote. And as a group, they cast even fewer ballots in "off-year," or non-presidential elections. The numbers speak for themselves, the participation of 18- to 24-year-olds was close to 50 percent in 1972. Votes cast by the same group dropped to 32 percent by the 1996 presidential election and an abysmal 20 percent during the 1998 off-year election. Voter participation continues to drop despite innovations and incentives like the National Voter Registration Act of 1993 ("Motor Voter") and NYVRM activities.

Here are a few more statistics concerning youth voter turnout that reinforce the point:

- In 1992, only 38.5 percent of 18- to 24-year-olds voted, compared to 70 percent of people 60 or older.

- In 1996, people between the ages of 18 and 24 made up near-ly 13 percent of the electorate. But roughly 42 percent of this group registered to vote and only 20 percent actually cast a ballot.

Clearly, young people aren't staying informed or casting ballots at election time. So why don't they participate? According to recent studies, there is more than one answer for why young people shy away from the electoral process. It appears to be a combination of factors including, in order of importance: they feel that their vote makes no difference; they don't have enough candidate information; they don't have enough time; the mud-slinging among political candidates and their surrogates turns them off; they dislike politics and protest by not voting; and they see little meaningful difference between candidates.

Clearly, factors of cynicism and apathy that are typically used to explain away this lack of participation are only part of the problem. In the end, many young people just don't feel a connection to the civic process or government. Or worse, they don't see a role for themselves in that process. We'll examine this concept further in coming chapters.

Chapter 20

Young America's Civic Engagement and Volunteerism

The previous chapter teed up the notion that today's young people are less involved in the electoral process than any other generation of youth in American history. It provided an introduction — a snapshot — of the problem's magnitude and some of its causes. This chapter seeks to provide a similar overview of America's youth in regards to their engagement in the larger civic process — specifically through volunteerism.

America's youth have shifted their activism from the political to the social realm. A 1992 Independent Sector survey found that more than half of all 18 to 24 year-olds volunteered during the previous year. But while 50 percent may seem like a significant number, America's modern youth are less active in volunteerism than other generational cohorts. It appears that their rationale or impetus for participation in the civic process is also much different than that of older Americans. In many instances, today's young people volunteer because it is mandated in their high school's curriculum, or because they see it as the only way to influence society or to make their voices and issues heard.

A recent Civic Education Study by the International Association for the Evaluation of Educational Achievement (IAEEA) compared the participation of America's youth to similarly aged people in other developed nations around the world. The study included: Canada, France, Russia, Mexico, Germany and Japan, among others. Interestingly, American 14-year-olds participated at higher rates in student government, youth political and environmental organizations, community-related volunteer groups, and charities collecting money for social causes than the 27 other countries participating in the study. American students participated at the same level as other nations in human rights organizations. And only seven nations outperformed the United States on engagement in civic organizations. So America's young people — those living in the modern cradle of freedom and democratic governance — only slightly outperformed children in places like Russia, where democracy is a fledgling phenomenon.

It's noteworthy that America's young people are fairly active in their schools and local communities. They join clubs, take interest in local issues and give their time to make a difference. Yet, in only a few years, when eligible to vote, these same children turn away from the larger community and the civic and electoral processes. **This is an important concept and a central element of this book's argument — young people are involved when the process matters to their daily lives.**

In other words, young people care about their prom theme or the rules that govern their school. They have a stake in the outcome of the decisions made by their peers in positions of influence, leadership and power. But perhaps more importantly, they take part because they feel their actions can make a difference, that their voice will be heard. But when taken to the larger community, where they perceive their influence is diminished, young people turn away and become disengaged.

Overall rates of volunteerism in America have risen during the past 25 years. While young people are slightly more likely to volunteer than the similar cohort 25 years ago, people 60 years of age or older are almost entirely accountable for the overall increase in service the past few decades. A 1996 phone survey of 1,500 people by the American Association of Retired People (AARP) found that 13 percent of 18- to 30-year-olds participated in "volunteer work," compared to 17.5 percent of people 71 or older. Obviously, the free time available to older Americans to volunteer is a significant reason for the discrepancy. However, as we'll see during this section of the book, it also has to do with a diminished understanding of civic responsibility among young people. As outlined previously, the diminished levels of volunteerism hold grave future consequences, as young people will be required to make greater contributions to offset the loss of our most active Americans, those of the Greatest Generation.

Chapter 21

A New World for America's Youth

Hopefully, the two previous chapters, while brief, provided a clear picture of the limited civic and electoral participation of America's youth. To better understand their disengagement, it might help to paint a caricature of "America's youth." For purposes of this book, we've defined young people as those between the ages of 18 to 30. They comprise Generations X and Y. The following chapters will examine the times these generations grew up in and the issues that shaped their views and outlook on life. And should provide a better understanding of exactly "who" Generations X and Y are, and why they choose not to participate in the civic process.

It's safe to say that on average, prior to 2000, members of Generations X and Y led charmed lives. They were unscathed by the traumatic experiences faced by their parents — events that defined the Baby Boomer generation. Other than the Gulf War, today's youth had faced no significant global conflict. The threat of nuclear war was diminished, and the economy boomed. But the world began to change significantly in the late 1990s.

The economy began to slow and events like Election 2000 and September 11th rocked the worldview of Generations X and Y. These drastic alterations in the way the world functioned provided a tremendous opportunity for young people to get involved. These events set the stage for a new "Greatest Generation," one that was forged by conflict, both global and interpersonal, and general adversity.

Newsweek dedicated an entire issue to evolving youth attitudes following 9/11. According to one of the students profiled, Greg Epstein, a 24-year-old graduate student at Michigan, "Our generation, as long as we've had an identity, was known as the generation that had it easy. We had no crisis, no Vietnam, no Martin Luther King, no JFK. We've got it now. When we have kids and grandkids, we'll tell them that we lived through the roaring nineties, when all we cared about was the number one movie or how many copies an album sold. This is where it changes…."

Both Generations X and Y were raised at a time of relative peace and prosperity with no major world events — until 9/11. Perhaps it was the relative ease of life that lessened the enthusiasm for active political engagement. Regardless, this inaction defined America's youth as masters of apathy when it came to political participation. That's a euphemism for saying that broad swaths of American society viewed the nation's youth as a bunch of "slackers." It's quite clear that many young people internalized this mantra and even found ways to celebrate it, by at worst flaunting their disengagement. And by at best, participating under the radar or in non-traditional civic pursuits.

Unlike their parents, Generations X and Y were confronted by few, if any widespread social or political movements that could have drawn them into the civic process. There was no Vietnam or Watergate to raise their collective blood pressure or spur their passions into action. As a result, a cadre of single issue or special interest group campaigns filled their void in the halls of government at every level. Also, during

Generation X and Y's lifetime, TV became a much more pervasive, omnipresent medium, beaming information 24-hours a day, seven days a week via cable and satellite. This bright media spotlight was trained, in large part, on entertainment and corruption or scandal, which limited in-depth political or issue analysis. Society became more interested in their leader's personal conflicts and tawdry scandals than the more profound issues that impact all of our daily lives.

It's hard to tell with any certainty which came first — the decline in prominence of political parties or the rise of 24-hour media — or perhaps, if one was a cause for the other. Either way, Generation X and Y grew up with political parties playing a much less prominent role in the electoral process. Campaigns became more about individual candidates and their platforms as parties faded into relative obscurity. Voters could no longer simply pull the lever for their party's candidates each election. Nor could they rely on candidates from their party sticking to tried and true messages or policy recommendations. Gone were well-defined, widely-embraced party platforms. Sound bites and rhetoric filled their void. The changing roles of political parties required voters to possesss greater political knowledge and sustained attention than ever before, making successful engagement more demanding.

Money also became a driving force in politics as campaign spending rose to record numbers and is still climbing. The 2004 election was the most expensive political contest of all time, as President Bush used his considerable war chest — more than any sitting president in history — to maintain control of America's governmental reigns. And Democratic nominee John Kerry — who unofficially received his party's nomination before virtually any non-sitting president in history — was forced to pull out every stop to compete with President Bush's elevated fundraising and spending. And the 2008 presidential election started earlier than any campaign in modern history. States front-loaded the primary election process — trying to steal the spotlight from New Hampshire and Iowa — which was a main reason candidates had to raise record sums of money just to compete.

It is this very type of political spending and financial influence that leads many young people to believe their voices are being drowned in the halls of government. And, as was discussed in section two of this book, the problem is compounded by a majority of young people believing that politicians have stopped reaching out to them for an opinion or a vote.

Most members of Generation X and Y are too young to remember the impact the economic collapse of the eighties had on their lives. But they remember quite well the investment explosion of the "dot-com" era. Members of Generation X left college commanding high salaries and cool perks. Employers courted them. For the most part, "Gen X" graduates had no idea what it was like to look for work or collect an unemployment check. They seamlessly moved from the classroom to the boardroom.

All of these factors combined to create an atmosphere that left little incentive or encouragement for two generations of America's youth to tune in to the events defining the world around them — particularly American politics.

The University of California Los Angeles' (UCLA) Higher Education Research Institute has tracked the civic attitudes of entering college freshman since the 1960s. Their numbers reinforce the notion that interest in politics has declined over time, bottoming out with generations X and Y. In the 2000 version of UCLA's annual study, only 28 percent of freshman followed politics compared to 60 percent in 1966 — a greater than 50 percent decline in less than 40 years!

Also of note, today's young people attend college in greater numbers than previous generations, graduating at much higher rates. But while more educated, they exhibit less civic acumen and possesss roughly the same to slightly less political knowledge than the similar cohort nearly sixty years ago. This runs counter to traditional indicators that say the higher a person's educational achievement, the greater their likelihood of being informed and active citizens. In a 2000 study, only 9 percent of America's youth reported having telephoned, written a letter or visited a government official to express views on a political issue — *that's less than one in ten*! Only 14 percent reported being interested in a political campaign — and that's in a presidential election year. And only 3 percent volunteered for a campaign, political party or participated in some form of organized protest.

Further, a 1998 study conducted by the National Assessment of Educational Progress found that nearly 75 percent of American high school seniors were not "proficient" in civics, even though they seem to have a basic understanding of government operation. For instance, 25 percent could not name two ways the Constitution prevents the president from becoming a dictator. Only 9 percent could list two ways a democratic society can benefit from citizen involvement. And only 30 percent understood that the power of judicial review protects the rights of individuals.

Clearly, Generations X and Y have limited interest in taking part in political activities or the civic process generally. According to recent attitudinal studies, civic participation is their lowest priority, far behind having a close-knit family; gaining knowledge, education and skills and finding a successful career. These are all important pursuits and young people should be commended for placing such importance on family and education. However, civic participation is a cornerstone of the "American family," and we will fail to solve our disputes and problems without significant (current and future) participation from these generations.

The truth is that most young people just don't believe or feel that government has any relevance to their daily lives. And even if these generations find an issue being debated in government that held meaning for them, many believe that they can't alter the outcome of the political process or make their voices heard. According to a 2000 Harvard University study, roughly 60 percent of college students believed that the major problems of our day will be solved through volunteerism, not by engaging in the government process.

It's hard to blame young people for feeling this way if you simply look at the major issues discussed in Congress and on TV each day. Besides the War on Terror and the economy, Congress most frequently addresses issues like shoring up Social Security, Medicare, universal healthcare and developing a prescription drug benefit for seniors. These issues don't even remotely resemble those identified in a 2000 study — "Y Vote 2000" — as having meaning to young people. According to the survey, respondents cared about protecting the environment (49 percent), providing health care for the uninsured (46 percent), working to reduce racial tensions (46 percent) and strengthening gun control laws (45 percent). Upon closer inspection, these issues focus on the larger world and problems in the global community.

Members of Generations X and Y came of age in a time of great globalization, in which technology reduced boundaries and brought people closer together. This is the newly adopted idea of the flattening world — and it is changing the way our young people view and participate in it. As a result, America's young professionals and teenagers care less about parochial "American issues" and would rather focus on solving global problems — something Congress rarely discusses (other than the War on Terror).

But as I tell young folks in my speeches and presentations, their civic inactivity is directly to blame for elected officials' propensity to discuss the issues of older Americans more than theirs. This is true because young peoples' voices are diminished in a government where 80 percent of 80-year-olds vote and only 20 percent of 20-year-olds take part. This mantra succinctly explains why elected officials talk with and listen to people that actively vote or engage in the civic process.

I sat on a panel a few years ago where an Atlanta City Councilman put it this way. If two people were waiting to see him about an issue or concern and there was only a small amount of time for meetings, the councilman would find out which one is the active voter and talk with that person. It is the voter who has taken the time to get informed, to get engaged. And ultimately, it is that person who helped him get elected, and could also help remove him from office.

With the exception of Bill Clinton in 1992, a significant portion of young Americans believe it is very unlikely an elected official will reach out to, or connect with them. According to former Rock the Vote Communications Director Cari Rudd, "Young people are sort of forgotten by our politicians. Politicians speak in a way that is not appealing to young voters."

Perhaps one of the starkest differences between modern youth and their predecessors is a lessened idealism. According to a recent Wall Street Journal study, in the 1960s, 80 percent of college freshman held developing a meaningful philosophy of life as their most important mission. Being financially well-off ranked fifth or sixth. By contrast, modern young people see the world in the complete opposite manner. More than 70 percent held being financially well-off as their top value, while the importance of developing a meaningful philosophy of life ranked sixth. Today's youth also value self-fulfillment above patriotism or religion. But to their credit, and perhaps contrary to their "slacker" image, generations X and Y are prepared to work hard for their individual successes.

Overall, young people hold ambivalent views of politics and their role in it. Roughly 50 percent say that voting matters, while 49 percent say it is "a little important" or "not at all." Only a fifth of modern young people see voting as a responsibility and less than 10 percent see it as a duty of citizenship. Think about that: less than 10 percent of America's youth fully-understand and endorse the responsibilities that go hand in glove with the benefits of being a citizen. Young peoples' ambivalence clearly carries over into their attitudes about larger civic participation. Roughly 46 percent believe they can at least make some difference, while 52 percent say they can make "just a little difference, almost no difference or no difference at all."

Further complicating any solution to diminishing youth participation, overwhelming numbers of young people see politics and elections as the business of "White Collar individuals," according to the *Wall Street Journal* survey. Almost half of young people believe elections are about politicians' personal interests and desire to beat the competition. Only 41 percent say it is about debating laws and issues, and a mere 32 percent say politics and elections are the way average Americans have their say in government.

Specific reasons for the declining civic participation of America's youth were addressed in previous chapters. And hopefully these recent chapters provided a clear understanding of how severe the civic crisis is among America's youth. America has two young cohorts, Generations X and Y, that overwhelmingly believe government is irrelevant to their daily lives, and at best, is a place where they have very limited power. That is, assuming they want to get involved and influence the process in the first place.

Chapter 22

Who is Generation X?

The previous chapter provided an overview of youth attitudes towards politics, government and the civic process. But in order to create solutions that will stop declining participation, we must clearly identify the attributes of each group — generations X and Y — differentiating between their backgrounds, interests and needs. While close in age, the two groups were shaped by different events, like the pervasiveness of e-mail, blogs, cellular technology and other advances. One is moving rapidly through adulthood, while members of Generation Y are still in their teens and early twenties. As a result, they are more susceptible to a change in attitudes and behavior.

This first chapter will take a closer look at Generation X, which consists of roughly 46 million members — the smallest generational cohort in America. They are traditionally considered those people born between 1965 and 1978. And they are moving beyond the moniker of young people, becoming adults with families, jobs and the responsibilities that traditionally begin to foster greater political activity and awareness.

Members of Generation X are very adept at using technology, having grown up playing with the first video game systems — enjoying an evolution from pong to Pac-Man to the more complex PlayStation games in the late nineties. This group was the first to widely use e-mail and the Internet on campus. They were also the first youth consumers of cable television, and were around when MTV was launched with the airing of the aptly titled song, "Video Killed the Radio Star." Technology had a lasting impact on this group's lives, shaping their civic involvement and connectedness to the world around them.

For many in Generation X, the 1992 elections were the first chance for political activism. It was certainly the first major political event they could take part in and ownership of in a meaningful way. And thanks to the candidacy of Bill Clinton, it was the first time many young people saw the relevance of government in their daily lives. It was the initial instance where they felt a politician was not only talking to them, but also discussing critical issues *with* them.

As described in this book's introduction, I am part of Generation X, and was moved by the power of Bill Clinton's message. I felt invited into the system and, for the first time, was optimistic about my power to influence government and to change the world. Many of my generational peers also felt this way in 1992, which led to the greatest youth voter participation in any presidential election since the 1970s, when 18-year-olds first earned the right to vote.

Also throughout the '90s, organizations like Rock the Vote and programs like MTV's Choose or Lose directly tried to engage young people in the political process. As previously discussed, these efforts simultaneously articulated the importance of being involved and the power of young people, while trying to educate them about the issues and the political process. Their overall power of meaningful activation is limited but they changed the discourse and perception of the process for Generation X.

And perhaps most notably, it was Bill Clinton's initial inspiration and emphasis on domestic projects like AmeriCorps and City Year that spurred a rebirth of service. These programs allowed members of Generation X to make actions speak louder than words through volunteer service at the local level — teaching in schools, providing brains and brawn to non-profit organizations and engaging in a host of other socially responsible activities. Generation X viewed these programs in the same way that their parents saw the Peace Corps — both generations ultimately heeding the call to action.

Again, as pointed out earlier, many young people believed these organizations were their only opportunity to make a difference, their one chance to bring about a better world because they didn't believe it was possible to get a foothold in the political process. And in large part, as a result of this political emphasis and inspiration, Generation X volunteers at slightly higher levels than members of Generation Y.

Generation X's view of politics, specifically their disinterest in the process, was also shaped by the political scandals of the Clinton years and the partisan tone of 1994's Republican "Contract with America." One of the most poisonous, partisan and problematic times in American political history was ushered in by the "Contract's" efforts to reshape government and its priorities. Politics in the 1990s was marked by personal attacks and a focus on issues that ran counter to the values and needs of young people.

Overall, 1994 was a time of vicious political bickering that created a negative view of politics and politicians for young people (and many Americans in general) that ultimately reversed the increased electoral participation of recent years. Personal scandals also diminished President Clinton's ability to push the agenda outlined during his campaign that had moved and inspired a generation. This seemed to reinforce young peoples' dismay with the process and dashed their hopes that President Clinton would truly change Washington's power structure by addressing issues they held close to their hearts and allowing them to shape the world in their image. And as a result, the damage done by the partisan and poisonous Clinton years led to the worst youth voter turnout for a presidential election in American history. Only 32 percent of 18- to 24-year olds cast a ballot in 1996.

Like their parents, members of Generation X experienced the possibilities of politics, only to be confronted by the current reality of partisanship and rhetoric. And on some levels, the tone in Washington justified an exodus from the political process for many "Gen Xers." They turned instead to volunteerism or the pursuit of personal financial reward during the roaring nineties and the dot.com era. Many young people hoped to make their mark on the world and a difference in the community outside of the mainstream political system.

Chapter 23

Who is Generation Y?

Generation Y is a unique collection of individuals who've grown up in the most modern of eras. Gen Y is comprised of people born between 1976 and 1995, and totals nearly 70 million individuals, which is almost as large as America's biggest group, the Baby Boomers. They also comprise the largest teen population in American history.

Generation Y, also known as the Echo Boomers, Boomlets, Millenials, Nexters, or the Net Generation, are the most technically savvy generation, having grown up with digital TV, PCs, ATMs, VCRs, DVDs, cell phones, pagers, laptops, elaborate video game systems, etc. Individuals in this generation tend to seek work environments that provide flexible hours, friendly atmospheres, a level playing field and ethical practices.

The Millenials were confronted with serious issues earlier in life than other generations of teens — crack cocaine, AIDS, gratuitous sex and violence on TV, etc., and as a result are more street-savvy and hardened, especially as consumers. But also as a result, they are very self-aware and less naïve than most generations at the teen and young adult stages of life.

I will never forget giving a speech on civic participation a number of years ago, to students of an affluent Atlanta private high school. I was invited to sit in on a student town hall being held before the talk. This was a campus-wide event, run by members of the student government. The gathering started out much as you'd expect, with discussions of homecoming, parking issues and local neighborhood opposition to the school's proposed sports facility improvements.

But what happened next thoroughly caught me off-guard, even though as a self-proclaimed pop culture aficionado, TV programs like "Dawson's Creek" and the "The O.C." aren't foreign programming. I'll even admit to being drawn in by their wit, sarcasm and discussion of prescient topics. If you've seen these programs, you know they portray their young protagonists as uber-wise, self-aware teens who oftentimes, "out-mature" their parents. The adult-themed subject matter and the witty banter between the young characters make you forget the actors are supposedly teens in average, small town America. I never believed teens actually thought or talked that way. That is, until I had the opportunity to observe this high school town hall meeting.

I was simultaneously amazed and saddened. The students' discussion moved from school dance logistics to an in-depth conversation about community acceptance and some students' ability to integrate into the small, seemingly elite group of young people on campus. The conversation took place in 2002, not far removed from the events of September 11. The discussion centered on issues of diversity and the community's ability to look beyond color, ethnicity and nationality to focus on the content of an individual's character. The most amazing part of this discussion was not only the elevated understanding of complex issues of multiculturalism — gender, race and diversity — but also the students' ability to easily communicate in a mature manner, while using a litany of multi-syllabic terms you'd expect to hear on "Crossfire" but not at a high school town hall meeting. It was instantly clear that folks at the former WB Network (producers of "Buffy the Vampire Slayer," "Dawson's Creek," "Gilmore girls" and other shows catering to 16- to 24-year-olds) had actually nailed their portrayals of young America.

But this group of Atlanta students wasn't finished. They moved from a discussion of ethnic diversity to one about sexuality and the campus's willingness to accept different preferences and orientations. Looking back on my high school days, I can't recall one instance where we had an open discussion of sexuality. Yet here were about 150 students openly talking about their preferences and issues like homosexuality and bi-sexuality. I found the students' maturity and eloquence truly impressive.

And it is that very fact — the deep comprehension of these topics and the relative ease with which these students discussed them — that saddened me. This auditorium contained a microcosm of America's youth (albeit an affluent segment), talking like a bunch of hardened adults, dealing with issues well beyond their years. If you closed your eyes, it would have sounded like a very frank and informed classroom discussion on a respected college campus — not something you'd hear in high school. Perhaps more aptly, it would have sounded like a less R-Rated conversation between the *Sex and the City* women.

I walked away from the experience fearing that our society was asking too much of young people on so many levels. I suddenly was empathetic with the stereotypical suburban mother who claims our children are being exposed to too much at an early age. It was also a bit frightening to realize I was getting old! Besides their outward appearance and subsequent discussions more fitting of young kids as they left the town hall, I was struck by this group of teenagers, most of whom were world-weary well beyond their years. They had seen and heard too much. And perhaps to an extent, they were robbed of their childhood.

That's why the outcome of my research on Generation Y was so surprising. While they have been exposed to so much at an early age, and outwardly appear to be impacted by these experiences, members of Generation Y are actually more optimistic than members of Generation X. Let's turn to pop culture for an example: Today, boy band graduates, newly crowned American Idols and Brittany Spears clones dominate the musical landscape — not the hardened angst of edgy bands like Nirvana, Sound Garden and Pearl Jam that members of Generation X revered. But while more optimistic about life in general, these formative experiences have led members of Generation Y to become skeptical of government institutions and the corporate world in large part because many of their company-dedicated parents were laid off or severely impacted by downsized salaries. And they were also bombarded with commercials through every conceivable medium.

The Boomlets are technically fluent multi-taskers who are flexible and team-oriented. They are also impatient and have short attention spans, with a need for instant gratification. Gen Y grew up in a digital, multimedia age with cellular phones, satellite TV and radio and the Internet, which provides information in quick snippets or bites. If not, consumers surf to the next site or channel until they are stimulated again.

This constant search for information and entertainment created an advertising paradise, where shoe, soda and clothing companies bombard kids with sales pitches and commercials. As a result, Boomlets are skeptical of slogans and marketing appeals and require more personal approaches to influence their decisions. One expert accurately called these young people a generation of "Type 'A' stress puppies."

It's truly difficult to tell which came first — advertisers or the significant spending habits of America's youth. Boomlets spend more than any other generation of young people in history, totaling nearly $141 billion in 1998 (that's $84 per week, per American teen). Therefore, many experts also call Generation Y the "choice generation." They have tremendous options — from types of water and soda, to jobs, educational opportunities and ways to spend their free time.

Take a moment to reflect back upon your childhood. How many soda options did you have? Who were the big footwear manufacturers? These days, young people can choose from dozens of sodas, coffees, waters, and various flavors of milk, in stores and at school. And they can put Nike, Adidas, Sketchers, Simple, Converse, New Balance or literally hundreds of other manufacturers' products on their feet. It's little wonder they are constantly looking towards the next fad and flexing their financial muscle by frequently purchasing an array of products.

Perhaps most interestingly, members of Generation Y also care about traditional values like stability and honesty, and they place significant importance on maintaining a close-knit family. They crave emotional fulfillment and personal balance in large measure because they are a generation of divorced latchkey kids who spent more time in front of the TV and computer than any other generation. Therefore, many are looking to build personal connections that were missing from their childhoods.

Yet members of Generation Y perform terribly when it comes to active citizenship. The 1998 National Association of Secretaries of State survey of 15- to 24-year-olds found that this generation has only a vague understanding of what it means to be a an active American citizen. More than half of the survey respondents placed a high value on "being an American," but few could offer any insight into what that means or requires. The Boomlets have a better understanding of citizen rights than they do of citizen responsibilities. Survey respondents' answers often included vague explanations of "helping others" and "being a good citizen." Ultimately, these young people do not see a role for themselves in the political process, nor do they see a connection to government and their daily lives. And their responses reflect the importance of slogans, not substance derived from the excessive advertising and media bombardment experienced from an early age.

Chapter 24

Election 2000: Events That Should Have Educated and Mobilized

The previous chapters painted a picture of youth disenchantment and disengagement with the American political process. Today's youth see little reason to engage in the civic process, nor do they possess an understanding of the numerous ways they can impact an election or the outcome of a political debate. The goal of this book is not to simply point out the negative, or paint a picture of America's decaying civic process. On the contrary, this book's main goal is to describe the current civic landscape, so that together we can understand the issues and mechanisms that turn people onto the process and help them appreciate the power they have to affect change. And so that together, we can engage our friends, family, co-workers and others in the civic process and share the rewards of becoming active citizens.

One of the places this change is most needed is with youth electoral participation. Too many young people believe they can't sway outcomes in the civic process by participating. Specifically, they do not see a direct connection between their ballot and the outcome of an election, and they are prone to ask whether "one vote can really make a difference." The closeness of the 2000 presidential election should have provided potential voters with a clear understanding of just how important each and every vote is to an election's outcome.

Actually, the 2000 election provided more than just the notion that every vote counts. It also helped Americans learn more about the workings of our political system. The extensive media coverage showed just how unique and special the American form of government is from anything around the world. The Founding Fathers created a system more than 200 years ago that foresaw the possibility of close contests like the one in 2000. And it was this vision that led them to create a system that withstood one of the most serious challenges in American history.

While people quibble about the election's outcome based upon whether their candidate won or lost, they don't argue about whether a declared winner was an inevitable outcome. Citizens knew a winner would be announced and our government would continue working. In other nations around the world, tanks would have rumbled down the streets to maintain order amid the immediate uncertainty following the election. We simply need to look at recent elections in the Ukraine and Mexico as evidence of that assertion. People would have rioted; chaos and terror would have ensued; and, most likely, lives would have been lost. But the procedures and processes that exist in America promised a certain if delayed, transfer of power from one president to the next.

And the media provided a front row seat to the civic process throughout the legal wrangling of Election 2000. The scrutiny and relentless coverage provided each of us with an imminently deeper understanding of how it all worked. And, in the end, the process did work. A majority of Americans agreed to support George W. Bush when he was sworn in as President of the United States of America.

But more importantly for the big picture of this section of the book, the 2000 election provided one of those potentially defining moments for America's youth. It was a moment like those that shaped the Greatest Generation — one that should have educated and mobilized a new generation to civic action. Unfortunately, subsequent chapters will show that this event didn't bring about new activity. But before moving to an analysis of youth engagement directly following the election, we need to take a closer look at the events of the battle for the White House to develop a better understanding of the significant role this could have (and should have) played in shaping young peoples' civic attitudes and actions. The following chapter examines the events of November and December 2000, which included excessive political rhetoric and numerous court challenges.

According to the Federal Elections Commission, overall voter turnout was actually slightly higher in 2000 than during the 1996 Presidential Election. Nearly 70 percent of the voting-aged population was registered and 59 percent of those people actually cast ballots, compared to 58 percent in 1996.

It was clear from the outset of Election Day — November 7, 2000 — that the contest would be unbelievably close. And it remained tight as the day wore on, elevating the importance of several "battle ground states" whose ballots wouldn't be counted until late into the evening. Florida was shaping up to be a particularly close contest. However, by 8 p.m. (EST) all the major networks had declared Vice President Al Gore the winner in Florida. This early declaration by the networks caused quite a stir, as they had to recant them later on that evening. Florida took center stage as election returns began solidifying in other states. Election experts and TV "talking heads" began elevating the importance of Florida's outcome, claiming that the entire election would be decided there — whoever won that state would move into the White House.

Based on close and late ballot returns in Florida, the election was too tight to call, even in the early morning of November 8. This set the stage for court battles and the chaos that ensued. By 2:15 a.m., the major networks had all reversed their earlier calls and were now awarding Florida's electoral votes to Governor George W. Bush. Reporters and the networks covering Florida predicted that the contest would be decided by more than 50,000 votes. Hearing this, Vice President Gore called Governor Bush to concede the election.

About 45 minutes later, Gore campaign staffers began hearing rumblings that the election was going to be much closer than recent calculations, so they encouraged their candidate to delay a public concession. Shortly thereafter, Vice President Gore called Governor Bush again, this time to rescind his concession. The call was heated and might have been partially to blame for the bloody battle that would ensue during the next month. At roughly 4:15 a.m., the networks again pulled their predictions as Florida's outcome tightened.

The chaos in Florida was compounded when questions began surfacing about the accuracy of votes cast in Palm Beach County, where third party candidates received higher than expected support. The questions over the Palm Beach ballots raised suspicions that there could have been a problem with the "butterfly ballot," which places names on the left and right sides of a punch hole column. Experts speculated that the ballots did not line up properly, leading to erroneous recordings of voters' intentions. Both candidates rallied quickly, sending teams of lawyers and election experts to Florida to watch the vote counting process, and to intervene with legal actions if necessary. As provided by Florida law, the closeness of the election automatically triggered a recount of the ballots. And in the process, the word "chad" began entering the American consciousness, perhaps burning itself into our brains forever.

Americans awoke on the 8th to confusion, speculation and political uncertainty. Television and radio programs were completely focused on the election and its uncertain outcome. On November 9, Vice President Gore tapped former Secretary of State Warren Christopher to lead his Florida legal team shortly after requests for hand recounts surfaced in Palm Beach, Dade, Broward and Volusia counties. Meanwhile, a circuit judge halted Palm Beach County's certification process, allowing time for a recount.

The events of November 10 only solidified the confusion in Florida. The state completed a machine recount of ballots, and the results — as gathered by the Associated Press — showed that Governor Bush led Vice President Gore by a mere 327 votes out of some six million cast across the state — only 300 or so votes!

On November 12, Palm Beach and Volusia County officials voted to recount their ballots by hand. As a result, the Bush team, led by former Secretary of State James Baker, filed a challenge to the county votes in federal court. Numerous lawsuits at the state and federal levels, from both parties, began surfacing during the following days and weeks. The lawsuits sought a range of remedies, including the halting of recounts and access to inspect ballots by hand.

Confusion and speculation was rampant across the country at this point, as the realization sunk in that this was an unprecedented event in American history. The urgency surrounding recounts and court challenges hit a fever pitch when Florida Secretary of State Katherine Harris vowed to deny certification for ballots that arrived in her office after the existing November 14 deadline. Vice President Gore's legal team responded to Harris' statement with the threat of a legal challenge. Meanwhile, a federal judge ruled against the Bush campaign's motion to stop the manual recounts taking place across Florida.

Counties all over the state would stop and start recounts during the following days. By way of example, Palm Beach County officials voted to temporarily halt the recount on November 14, while Dade County began a limited examination of roughly one percent of "questionable" ballots in a handful of precincts. In the end, Secretary of State Harris conceded and extended the certification deadline to 2 p.m. (EST) on November 15.

Secretary Harris held firm to the decision not to accept ballots delivered to her office after 2 p.m. on the 15th. And she asked the Florida State Supreme Court to halt all on-going manual recounts. At the same time, Broward County officials decided that a hand recount was necessary and the Associated Press announced that the Bush lead in Florida had dropped to a miniscule 286 votes. Think of how close that is — 286 votes out of nearly six million cast! All the while, media talking heads continued their speculation about the election's outcome. And their detailed discussions and "Monday morning quarterbacking," were providing amazingly detailed explanations of each legal and political step.

November 16 was a prime example of the legal chess game playing itself out in courtrooms at every level of the American judicial system. The Bush legal team submitted a written argument to the U.S. Federal Appeals Court in Atlanta requesting a halt to all ongoing Florida recounts. This led the Democrats to file a counter suit in the same court. Meanwhile, on the same day, the Florida Supreme Court decided to allow the Palm Beach County recount.

On November 17, the Florida Supreme Court sent notice to Secretary Harris that she was not allowed to certify the election until they ruled on the Democrats' motion pending in their court. Simultaneously, Miami-Dade County reversed its original decision and commenced a full manual recount. And the 11th Circuit Court denied the Bush team's request to halt the recount on Constitutional grounds. The following day, absentee ballots were opened and counted, and estimates surfaced that Governor Bush was leading Vice President Gore by 930 votes.

If it seems like this chapter is an ebbing and flowing story, think about the chaos on TV, in the paper, on the radio and around water coolers at that time! Chaos continued on November 21, when the Florida Supreme Court supported the ongoing hand recounts, setting a five-day deadline for their completion. As a direct result, many counties suspended their recounts out of fear that they couldn't complete them in time for the recently-set Supreme Court deadline. Miami-Dade County officials halted their recount, dashing some of the Gore team's hopes of higher vote totals from heavily Democratic precincts.

Not satisfied with the Florida Supreme Court's decision to continue the recounts, the Bush team took their case to the highest court in the land, filing motions with the U.S. Supreme Court in Washington, D.C., on November 24. The nation's top judicial body agreed to hear the Bush appeal on the Florida Supreme Court ruling that allowed recounts to continue. The events of November 26 added a personally partisan tone to the proceedings when the Florida Supreme Court's deadline passed, which allowed Secretary Harris to certify the election. The totals gave Governor George W. Bush a slim 537-vote victory over Vice President Al Gore. Many Gore supporters saw the outcome, and Secretary Harris' role in it as political, considering that George W. Bush's brother Jeb, was governor of Florida.

The partisan rhetoric hit a fever pitch when news surfaced that Secretary Harris did not count ballots from Palm Beach County because they arrived two hours after her deadline. President-elect Bush seized the opportunity, trying to cement the outcome in the minds of the American people by announcing that his transition team would immediately plan its move into the White House. But the Gore team didn't yield, filing a motion to overturn Harris' decision on November 27 in the Florida courts. Trying to avoid being drawn into the political

tempest, the federal General Services Administration — which allo-
cates funds for the presidential transition team — announced that it
would withhold money to either candidate for the transition process
until the election dispute and its court actions were resolved.

The next day, Judge N. Saunders Saul was selected to hear the
Gore team's motion. He set a December 2 hearing on the case, and
required that all Palm Beach and Miami-Dade County ballots be sent
to Tallahassee (where his court was located) in case an inspection was
necessary during the hearing. The shipment of these delicate ballots,
with their loose, pregnant and hanging chads, was quite an undertaking considering more than one million votes were cast in those two
counties alone.

As part of the presidential election process, the winning candidate
in each state receives "delegates," or citizens who will vote for them
in the Electoral College. Each state legislature is required to select its
electors shortly after each presidential contest. So on November 30,
the Florida legislature voted along party lines to hold a special session, if necessary, to identify electors if the contest wasn't decided by
December 12 — less than a week before the Electoral College was
scheduled to meet.

The United States Supreme Court began its hearing on December
1, to decide whether the Florida Supreme Court acted within its powers
by ordering Secretary Harris to include manual recounts in Florida's
election certification. Again, the following days were filled with a rush
of action, which was oftentimes conflicting. While the U.S. Supreme
Court began its hearings, the Florida Supreme Court upheld Judge
Saul's decision to halt manual recounts.

And on December 4, after two days of hearings, Judge Saul ruled
against Vice President Gore. The ruling stated that the Gore team's arguments "didn't prove that the manual recounts would change the certified outcome." Gore's lawyers immediately filed an appeal with the

Florida Supreme Court, while the U.S. Supreme Court simultaneously asked the Florida court to explain its ruling that allowed the recounts in the first place. In other words, the U.S. Supreme Court would not act on the matter until Florida's high court clarified its position.

On December 7, the Florida Supreme Court commenced hearing the Gore challenge to Judge Saul's ruling. The next day (by a four-to-three vote) the Florida Supreme Court reopened the election, allowing the recounts to continue in counties with significant "undervotes." The Bush legal team immediately appealed the decision to the U.S. Supreme Court, seeking an injunction that would prevent the recounts from starting. Meanwhile, the Florida Legislature met in special session to select the state's delegates to the Electoral College, which would convene in a little more than one week.

All legal challenges had been exhausted at the state level, and the final stage was set on December 9, when the U.S. Supreme Court (by a five to four decision) ended all Florida recounts so that they could hold hearings on the matter. The court began their hearings two days later with the Bush team presenting its case stating that the Florida Supreme Court again overstepped its bounds by allowing the recount to start a second time. The Gore team countered with arguments that the U.S. Supreme Court had no jurisdiction in the case, and no legal right to halt the Florida recount.

The 35 days of debate, political sniping and court challenges came to an end on December 12. The U.S. Supreme Court ruled in favor of the Bush team. Their decision stopped all ongoing recounts in Florida, which ultimately allowed Secretary Harris' certified results to stand. Governor George W. Bush received Florida's 25 electoral votes, giving him a 271 to 267 victory in the Electoral College, where 270 votes are needed to win.

Chapter 25

The Media's Election Tutorial

The fight for the White House was rancorous, with both sides assembling teams of lawyers, volunteers, political operatives and experts who descended on Florida to monitor the recount process, challenge decisions in court, and ultimately creating a disruptive environment for the system as a whole. Both campaigns used venomous language to describe the other side's efforts and made public accusations about questionable, even illegal activities, by the people representing each camp. The media covered every legal challenge, rhetorical barb and breaking development in the battle for the White House in striking detail. In the end, this exhaustive media coverage provided average citizens with an important opportunity to learn about their government, its laws and its electoral system.

Much of what Americans saw, read and heard in the coverage of the 2000 election presented a less than positive portrayal of our electoral and court processes. Many people who had not previously followed politics did follow the ensuing controversy only to confirm their belief that our system isn't perfect and does have some warts. But ultimately, the exact opposite was true. Americans should have concluded that our system of government, which was successfully designed more than 230 years ago, withstood even the toughest of challenges. No matter what candidate they supported, most Americans walked away from the extended election process better informed and more confident that the system does indeed work. And frankly, it worked in a way that no other form of government around the world, or in history, can match.

Absent from the election news coverage were images of tanks rolling down the streets to secure government buildings from looters or protesters. Americans were not confronted with news of any coup, or assassination attempts of candidates or the sitting president. On the contrary, the courts, the Constitution and our legislative process decided the election's outcome without riots and bloody physical battles.

The system worked, because an overwhelming majority of Americans agreed to support the election winner, whether he was their candidate or not. Immediately following the Supreme Court's ruling, 80 percent of those polled said they would accept Governor Bush as president. Nearly 43 percent of those polled said they disagreed with the Supreme Court's decision, yet only 30 percent said the decision made them lose confidence in the process. And more than 65 percent said the Supreme Court's decision had no effect on their faith in the American judicial or political system.

Even Vice President Al Gore acknowledged the system's effectiveness and finality in his very brief concession speech. "Neither Governor Bush nor I anticipated this long and difficult road," he said. "Certainly neither of us wanted it to happen. Yet it came, and now it has ended, resolved as it must be through the honored institutions of our democracy," Gore said. "While I strongly disagree with the Supreme Court's opinion, I accept it."

It's amazing when you stop to think that a document written seemingly ages ago, could stand the test of time and ensure continuity of government operations even under the most stressful of challenges. It's breathtaking to contemplate that the authors of the Constitution — our nation's roadmap for democracy, freedom and representative rule — had the foresight to predict challenges like Election 2000 and to create a system that could withstand an army of lawyers (some of the brightest minds in our nation) and countless legal challenges.

Election 2000 did, however, illuminate the fact that the American electoral process is flawed in ways that required immediate tweaking in order to ensure more accurate counting of ballots and prevent future election disputes. As noted in previous chapters, many changes took place right after the election, a good number of them implemented by states in time for the 2004 elections. States are, and will surely continue to tweak their election systems as they work to meet the provisions of the resulting 2000 federal legislation.

The 35-day struggle for the White House appears to be a double-edged sword. As outlined earlier in this section, Americans, particularly the young and disenchanted, have a higher favorable opinion of government today than they did in 1998. They trust institutions to work more effectively. Yet, as will be evident from the election numbers that follow, the education of Election 2000 did little to change the political actions of young people.

Election 2000 reinforced another negative stereotype as well. Significant percentages of young people believe that elections are merely contests among individuals seeking power, in which personal opinions and hopes are deferred to the "system" and special interests. Many young people point to the fact that Vice President Gore was the first presidential candidate since 1888 to win the popular vote but lose the election as evidence that the system is beyond their control.

The 2000 Election and its subsequent media coverage presented some unequivocal benefits though too. Americans received a broad tutorial in the electoral process and gained greater insight into how our courts and legislative processes work. The protracted election and subsequent media coverage provided an opportunity for people to see not only how the system works, but that, even with warts, it *does* work. Remember, an overwhelming 80 percent of CNN poll respondents said they accepted George Bush as the legitimate president in January and 66 percent said that the Supreme Court's decision had no effect on their judgment or opinion of the system. The 2000 battle for the White House proved that people trust that our system of government will ensure the peaceful transition of leaders from election to election.

The election also disproved another commonly held belief. Members of generations X and Y and numerous other citizens choose not to be involved in the election process because "their vote doesn't matter." The common mantra is that one vote won't make a difference in an election's outcome. Yet the 2000 presidential election was decided by slightly more than 500 out of nearly six million votes in Florida. Those few hundred ballots gave Governor George W. Bush the votes necessary to win the Electoral College. It doesn't get any closer than that, and rarely have so few votes had such massive consequence in American politics.

The combination of the media tutorial and President Bush's razor thin margin of victory in Florida should have helped young people realize the importance of being involved in the process. It should have made them take action in the next election because they now understand our system better, and know that a small number of votes actually carries great power. But as the title of this chapter implies, Election 2000 didn't immediately change youth voter behavior. This paradox will be examined in future chapters. Results from the next election — 2004 — appear to have proven that Election 2000 also failed to create the next "Greatest Generation."

Chapter 26

September 11, 2001 Tests a Generation's Mettle

Study after study shows that significant numbers of Generations X and Y believe elected officials do not talk to them about issues of importance, if they engage them directly at all. Perhaps the greatest opportunity to rally young people came in the wake of the horrific events of September 11, 2001. The unconscionable acts of terrorism rallied Americans in all corners of the nation and from all walks of life to a newfound patriotism and compassion for "America" and its residents. What an opportunity to turn one of the most devastating events in American history into one of the greatest and longest-lasting triumphs — creating the next Greatest Generation.

Let us reflect on the days, months and years following 9/11 to get a clearer picture of the opportunity at hand. People felt a strong connection to those living in and close to New York City, Washington, D.C., and Pennsylvania. And many Americans had a direct connection to those sites — whether a friend worked in the Twin Towers or a loved one was a passenger on an ill-fated plane used in the attacks.

Stories about the determination, grit and endurance of first-responders (police, fire and medical professionals) searching the incident sites in the three locations filled the media. Americans everywhere were moved by the dedication these folks showed with their exhaustive searches to find survivors and continued efforts to squelch the flames in the rubble of the Pentagon, one of America's most recognizable buildings and the headquarters of our military and intelligence apparatuses. In typical fashion, Americans rallied.

Stories abound about New Yorkers delivering clean boots and clothes, toilet paper and soap to the former site of the Twin Towers so the workers could go about their grim jobs with some level of comfort and security. Countless local restaurants closed for business in order to feed the men and women who were continuing the rescue work. Americans in all corners of our country donated blood and gave money to victims' families and to the firefighters, police and EMS funds that sprang up in the days and months following the attacks.

People unable to directly lend a hand showed their support by wearing their patriotism on their sleeves — literally. Flags flew at homes and businesses where they had never flown before. Stickers with slogans of support and American flags covered bumpers and windows on highways and roadways in small towns and large cities. Celebrities organized phone-a-thons to raise money for the Red Cross; musicians wrote songs and held benefit concerts to support emergency workers. The point is this: patriotism was rampant, and Americans displayed their rekindled idealism in countless ways.

As candidate Bill Clinton was my generation's John Kennedy, the events of September 11, 2001 held the possibility of being Generation X and Y's Pearl Harbor. America's anger and vengeance was aroused on December 7, 1941, in Hawaii when the Japanese attacked our ships as they sat quietly in the harbor. The incident led us to war, just as the events of September 11 would. The Japanese attacks also brought a loud, passionate cry from a generation that would change the world forever and solidify America's position as the mightiest Super Power the world would ever know.

Similarly, the events of September 11 showed the promise of an attitudinal shift among America's youth. While 9/11 will never be forgotten, it appears not to have ultimately fueled a rebirth of civic action among America's youth. Raised flags did not translate into raised levels of civic action. This section of the book examines Generations X and Y's immediate response to the events of 9/11, their attitudes towards the War on Terror and protests over the war in Iraq.

Attitudes and Action Immediately Following 9/11

There was great confusion, concern and interest stirring on campuses from coast-to-coast in the days immediately following the terrorist attacks. It was nearly impossible for schools to continue running in a "business as usual" manner. Many changes were made to accommodate the devastation and profound loss felt by students on campuses all across America.

While it might seem trivial, a noteworthy sign of these changes was the cancellation of football games that tend to be near-sacred events at America's largest campuses. As University of Michigan President Lee Bollinger pointed out in a 2001 *Newsweek* article, time alone was not enough to return normalcy to campus life: "It became clear to all of us that the magnitude of this was so great that a few days would not separate ordinary lives from this event," Bollinger said. "People would need to regain ordinary life over a longer period of time."

The content of countless courses and the focus of campus activity changed drastically as well. There was a palpably elevated interest in terrorism and world events immediately following 9/11. For example, UCLA created 50 new courses for the fall semester as a direct result of the attacks, and nearly all of the offerings focused on "perspectives of 9/11" in some form or fashion. Students began packing forums and panels on Middle Eastern history, religion and politics. Local campus media began running international news as part of their normal content and faculty incorporated the events into ongoing class discussions. The events seemed to send students scrambling to understand what they should have already known about the world around them. Naturally, students also became concerned with the prospects of a military draft. And forums and articles on the topic began to appear regularly.

Sadly, but perhaps not unexpectedly, a current of anti-Arab and Muslim activity began flowing as well. Arab and Muslim students received threatening e-mails, were accosted in their dorms, and in general were discriminated against and distrusted based upon their appearance, name and/or religion. Some students tried policing their more aggressive peers by raising the understanding of the ethnic, religious and cultural differences in the Middle East. Student associations and other campus groups held teach-ins, rallies and speeches on religion, hate crimes, etc.

Patriotism was also in full roar during this time as college students from all political persuasions rallied to support President Bush — just like their adult counterparts. A November 2001 Newsweek Poll found youth attitudes matching most of America's: roughly 83 percent of young people approved of President Bush's job performance; and 85 percent agreed with military action in Afghanistan. Debates about whether the events of 9/11 would unite young people like Pearl Harbor in 1941, or divide the nation like Vietnam in 1966, were ongoing and passionate.

There was also a rising tide of appreciation for the military on campus, which was similar to the support that blossomed during World War II. As reported by *Newsweek*, a University of Michigan ROTC captain recalled a fitness run through campus with 23 of her fatigue-clad soldiers following 9/11. People actually cheered the passing cadets at points along their run. In one particularly poignant moment, people stopped on a bridge and started clapping. Before, these soldiers-in-training were yelled at for being another hassle students had to deal with on the way to class, if anyone paid attention to them at all. Now they were being celebrated and cheered. According to Captain Jessica Ryu, "It bothers me that it took so many people to die to make others proud to be an American. I felt that from day one."

September 11 also brought a change in the attitudes of young people toward government. Polls immediately following the events showed young adults were suddenly more trusting of government and its leaders. There also seemed to be an up-tick in interest surrounding community-based organizations or groups working to tackle important issues. Finally, the events also created a shift in professional interests and career paths for young people, as they began considering jobs in government, military, law enforcement and the medical community.

Newsweek focused a November 2001 article on John Jay College (part of the City University of New York), which is home to a leading criminal justice program. Admissions representatives immediately saw significantly increased interest in their programs in the days, weeks and months following the attacks. The presence of John Jay College at college fairs began actually drawing a crowd after 9/11. It seemed that students were responding out of patriotism, while also looking toward their futures. According to John Weidenfeld, a John Jay College admissions counselor, "Students who might have looked at chemistry or biology at another college three months ago are checking out our forensic-science program. Many of them want to know, 'Will John Jay prepare me for the FBI, Secret Service and INS,'" he said. A November 2001 *Newsweek* poll supported this theory, proving that significant numbers of young people believe careers in medicine (48 percent), the military (46 percent) and science/technology (44 percent) would be more popular in years to come.

Overall, America's youth attempted to pay greater attention to the world around them (at home and abroad) immediately following the events of 9/11. There was an increased pursuit of knowledge for the culture and climate of the Middle East. And a fresh perspective and respect blossomed for the military, government and its leaders. While the jury is still ultimately out, it appears that these horrific events failed to bring about deeper and sustained civic participation among America's youth. The events happened, and young people were affected and awakened in numerous ways outlined above. But they failed to take sustained civic action.

Sadly, the rise and fall of patriotism following 9/11 highlights another trend that has come to represent America's attitudes and responses to major events. The palpable, public enthusiasm surrounding the cause of "liberty" waned within a few weeks and months, as symbols came down and people's attention returned to issues in their daily lives. As we'll see from the 2002 and 2004 elections, all the newfound appreciation for the military and our government following the events of 9/11, failed to spur meaningful political or community action among young people. While the most recent studies show an increase in volunteerism and individual and corporate financial giving, overall voter registration and actual rates of participation are down. And young people today are no more inclined to see voting as an important act of citizenship.

Chapter 27

Attitudes About the War on Terror and Resulting Civic Action

We just learned that young people rallied to support government leaders, institutions and local community groups, while learning more about America's new, visible enemy immediately following 9/11. Yet their engagement, patriotism and interest waned as time passed — especially as national mourning and political unity were replaced with partisan carping and a march towards the War on Terror and a conflict in Iraq.

America's youth spawned a massive protest movement at home as the nation's military marched into a bloody war in Vietnam. An entire "make love, not war" culture developed that blended music, drugs and passionate protest on campuses and in cities from California to New York. The voices of today's youth were almost non-existent by comparison, even in the wake of the bloodiest terror attack in American history. Overall, the protests and anti-war activities of today's youth were miniscule compared to those in the Vietnam era. And the issues being debated differed as well.

Polls at the commencement of the War on Terror depicted the seemingly contradictory attitudes of young people toward civic participation. While interest and awareness in government debate and critical issues were up, overall civic participation levels remained relatively static. More than 70 percent of young people said that the War on Terror was at least somewhat more likely to make them participate in the civic process, yet only 35 percent said they were much more likely to participate immediately. And as outlined in the last chapter, young people trusted government more — yet that didn't result in greater interaction, whether in the form of phone calls to members of Congress supporting or opposing military action, or votes on Election Day. There was an elevated interest among young people in serving in law enforcement roles following 9/11 and at the start of the War on Terror. But fewer were willing to become soldiers in one of the four main branches.

Elected officials took a more prominent role in the American psyche following 9/11. Most Americans will recall the indelible images of government leaders responding to the tragedy: Mayor Rudolph Giuliani (who ran for president largely on the events of 9/11) walking the debris-strewn streets of lower Manhattan only hours after the attacks; President Bush, bullhorn in hand, commending the first responders at the attack site; and members of Congress standing united, singing "God Bless America" on the steps of the Capitol, in a gesture far beyond partisan bickering. These and countless other non-partisan actions are examples of our government's ability to rise above the political fray to rally support for America and our common good. And that, in large measure, is why more people trusted government and elected officials in the early part of the war.

Following 9/11, young people paid closer attention to national politics than at any time in decades. According to a Pew Charitable Trust survey, nearly 60 percent of young people said they were not "generally

bored with what goes on in Washington." As will be detailed in subsequent chapters, Americans tend to pay more attention to national
politics instead of issues at the state and local level. That's why turnout
in presidential elections is higher than in "off-year" contests. And the
Pew survey proved this attitude continued in the wake of 9/11. While
interest in Washington politics was up more than 15 percent among
young people from 2000, attention to local politics dropped about five
points, to a low of 45 percent.

Government leaders and institutions were certainly more visible
following 9/11, and Americans trusted both more. Yet they were not
anymore inclined to *take part* in government or run for office. Here
are some key facts:

- More than half (57 percent) of young people surveyed in late
  2001 said they were "not at all likely to run for office themselves," which spiked from 37 percent in 1998.
- Nearly 55 percent said they were "not at all likely to work for a
  political party."
- Exactly 50 percent said that they were "not at all likely to join a
  political group or organization."
- Less than 40 percent said they were "likely to volunteer on a
  political campaign."
- Roughly 44 percent said they were "not at all likely to march,
  protest or join a demonstration or rally."

And yet, even the stated intentions to participate in the civic process didn't translate into action in 2001. In fact, volunteerism and voter
registration rates dropped following 9/11 and at the start of the War
on Terror. A 2001 study by the Center for Democracy & Citizenship
found that roughly 66 percent of respondents claimed to be registered
to vote, which was down from 70 percent in 1998 and 2000.

Rates of student participation were down, and protest methods employed by the "War on Terror" era youth were, in large measure, different from Vietnam era tactics. The activities were much less visible to the average observer and relied upon an array of technology-based tools to organize events and send messages to "political decision makers." Peace protests were announced in the form of e-mail petitions on campus Intranets across America, instead of appearing as large rallies on the campus quad or administration steps. Sit-ins and civil disobedience were replaced by teach-ins, organized for the purpose of educating students about the different cultures, military actions and consequences of the War on Terror. Additionally, young Americans generally supported the War on Terror and military action in Iraq (at its beginning), which was quite a departure from the public and passionate protests over involvement in Vietnam.

According to a 2001 poll by Americans for Victory over Terrorism, young people were generally supportive of U.S. action in Afghanistan. More than 62 percent of respondents said that action in Afghanistan was moral, and only a little more than 20 percent felt it was immoral. More than 72 percent believed the war was "just," compared to only 15 percent who felt it wasn't. And an overwhelming percentage of students supported American attacks on Iraq if it was proven that Saddam Hussein was trying to build weapons of mass destruction. Nearly 70 percent of respondents believed the United States had the "right" to invade Iraq. And an overwhelming 78 percent of respondents believed that the United States had "the right to overthrow Saddam Hussein."

These numbers faded as the War on Terror and the prospect of action in Iraq turned into full-blown war with Saddam Hussein. According to a March 2003 Gallup poll, nearly 72 percent of Americans supported the war in Iraq, which differed sharply from college student opinions. Ivy League colleges and universities provide a snapshot of American campus attitudes because their student political leanings seem to cover the full-spectrum from school to school. Campus polls show that young people supported the war, on average, less than older Americans. Nearly 60 percent of Princeton students supported the war, as compared to only 47 percent of Columbia students and 35 percent of Harvard students. Princeton tends to be the most conservative of Ivy League institutions. And support for the war was fervent among the 60 percent who were in favor of action in Iraq. Exactly 50 percent said they "strongly supported" it and 50 percent said they "somewhat supported" it. Only 36 percent of Princeton students were against the war, and 16 percent of those felt there was "no justification for war without Iraq presenting an immediate threat to American security." Only 4 percent of students polled believed there "is never justification for war." Support for the war at Ivy League institutions included a range of justifications, including: "it was a battle of ideology; the creation of democracy in Iraq would serve as a model for other Arab nations; and the belief that the Hussein regime was harboring terrorists and possesssed weapons of mass destruction."

Interestingly, there was a deep current of support for the notion that "Saddam Hussein was a threat that needed to be dealt with," but many students wanted alternatives to the Bush plan. While they were troubled by the specter of Saddam Hussein, young people weren't convinced military action was the only way to handle him. And they certainly didn't believe that unilateral military action by the U.S. was the right approach. Nat Myers, a Harvard student was quoted in the school's paper as saying, "This is a conflict that probably should be fought…probably. If this war was going to be fought by the United Nations — rather than having the U.N. bullied into it by the U.S., it might be acceptable."

Youth distrust of government grew as memories of the 9/11 attacks faded and the war with Iraq loomed larger on the horizon. This manifested itself into skepticism about the United States' rationale for war and our ability to rebuild Iraq after the conflict, which is an important distinction from Vietnam era attitudes. At the start of Vietnam, there was little reason to distrust America's ability to win, or rationale for war considering we had successfully fought World War II and assisted with the reconstruction of Europe. By contrast, today's overwhelming youth propensity to distrust the American government's motive and ability to rebuild Iraq are, in large part, a direct result of Vietnam and the Watergate scandal.

Another important difference between today's protesters and Vietnam's is that many students believed protesting is futile because the war is inevitable anyway. Therefore, no amount of protesting will change the outcome from a government they see as disconnected from their views and uninterested in their input. As outlined earlier, today's youth cynicism toward government is a direct byproduct of Vietnam, Watergate and the Clinton years of political scandal and partisanship.

Campus protests were also much different leading up to the war in Iraq than they were during Vietnam. For example, the National Youth and Student Peace Coalition — comprised of 15 student groups who joined forces after 9/11 — organized a "Books not Bombs" protest around the country that drew, apparently intentionally, limited crowds at colleges and high schools. Their events at the University of California Los Angeles, University of Colorado and the University of Wisconsin drew roughly 1,000 students each. Only about 500 students turned out at the University of California Berkeley event, which was a hotbed of peace protests and civil disobedience during Vietnam.

The protest messaging was also different this time around. Protestors of the first Iraq conflict — the Gulf War — complained that America's actions were driven by a desire to protect our oil interests. And Vietnam-era language was based upon "peace and love," and a war that wasn't "justifiable." Today's college protestors articulated a much simpler and local message: The war would have few tangible positive outcomes. Most prominent was the idea that, "money used for the war would be taken from domestic priorities." Perhaps much of the talk came from students feeling the economic hardships of the post-9/11 economic downturn. State budget crunches led to cuts in university funding, which forced increases in tuition costs and decreases in the number of scholarships. Instead, young people opposed to the War on Terror wanted government funds and energies directed to solving domestic issues like this one that directly impacted their lives.

Regardless of the rationale for protesting, the War on Terror and the subsequent invasion of Iraq presented young people with an opportunity to make their voices heard. Rallies of support for the War on Terror were minimal, even though significant numbers of young people felt the military actions were appropriate, just or necessary at the outset. And protests against American military action were limited in frequency and tame compared to Vietnam activity. Rather than rising to meet the challenges growing around the world, overall involvement in the civic process continued to remain low among America's youth. All the fervor and concern was audible but merely bluster, as young people remained relatively disengaged from the civic process. Another opportunity to leave an indelible mark on the world through civic participation slipped through the fingers of America's youth in the wake of 9/11. Young people turned their back on the civic process and larger dialogue of world changing events to focus on individual pursuits, continuing the downward spiral of youth participation. If the most earth shattering event to take place on American soil didn't bring about a torrent of youth passion and action...what will?

Chapter 28

Volunteerism in a Post 9/11 World

A number of current studies show that rates of volunteerism and corporate philanthropy are on the rise in the United States. However, the state of volunteerism immediately following 9/11 reinforced a picture of Americans focused more on personal pursuits than improving the larger world around them. Traditionally, Americans volunteer more than citizens in any other nation in the world. According to a 2000 survey by Independent Sector, nearly 56 percent of Americans volunteer. According to the same study, Americans volunteer an average of 3.5 hours per week. Interestingly, many of the services managed by volunteers or nonprofit organizations in America are government-led elsewhere, which partially explains the discrepancy in participation rates between America and nations around the world.

Perhaps a great deal of the American ethic of looking out for others in our community can be traced back to the founding principle of "we the people." This notion is woven into the fabric of who we are as a nation. American "community service" took hold with the original settlers, who helped each other survive and succeed in a strange, inhospitable land. They faced the hardships of brutal weather, battles with indigenous peoples and discomfort in a land foreign to their European experience. American colonists were required to look after each other and work together if they hoped to prosper, let alone survive. In large measure, it was this ethos that allowed them to prosper. As a result, this interdependence and "community ethos" became a founding principle of life in the colonies, which cemented the underpinnings of our current government. And the emphasis on volunteerism continues today. The documents written by our Founding Fathers to prescribe how America would live, grow and be governed were created with a less powerful government in mind. This allowed for the creation of communities that sustained themselves through local rules and norms. As a result, Americans were more inclined to support each other instead of relying on government to sustain them.

Religious institutions have also played an important role in the development and nourishment of an American service ethos. These organizations consistently provide food, shelter and clothing in times of community need. Again, as dictated by the founders, government at all levels was to support organizations that provide the services to communities and individuals that they are incapable, unwilling or unchartered to support. Sometimes this takes the form of direct financial subsidies. And sometimes the support is human capital, like with AmeriCorps, Vista and City Year. This approach is very different from the efforts of government in other parts of the world.

Yet, volunteerism declined immediately following 9/11. And participation among young people has been on the decline for a number of years, even though it is often a mandated component of graduation from public school programs across the country. In a 2001 survey, roughly 70 percent of young people said they donated food, clothing or money to a church or community group in the past couple of years. This is actually down from the 86 percent who did so in 1998. According to the same study, joining a club or non-political organization was down 11 points from 1998, to 47 percent. And volunteering at homeless shelters or other community programs dropped 10 points since 1998, resting at 38 percent.

Rates of "episodic" volunteerism immediately following 9/11 were down even from the year before. Roughly 31 percent of poll respondents said they "volunteered at least once a year, but more like every two or three months," which is down 7 percent from the year before. And 37 percent of respondents said they "never volunteer," which is actually up 10 percent from 2000.

It is certainly understandable that people turned inward following 9/11 to focus on improving their own lives, which now seemed less impenetrable. The economy was in bad shape and people were losing jobs by the thousands. The average family found it more difficult to make ends meet. The job sector was particularly difficult and uncertain for young people, as they struggled to find work upon graduation in a very competitive marketplace. Also, the fear, confusion and increased distrust of our own neighbors and community members led many people to shy away from reaching out to others with assistance — or for help in their own lives.

Unfortunately, this reinforces the theme that many within Generations X and Y are turning away from civic participation for more singular pursuits. The Harvard study discussed earlier pointed out that young people believe volunteerism, and not being engaged in government, would solve the major problems of our day. Agreed, volunteerism is a critical component of solving societal ills. Yet government has the power to bring about change more swiftly with issues like education and the environment because it can marshal significant money and resources to attack a problem at its roots. That's why it is so troubling to see significant numbers of young people turning away from one of America's most powerful forces for positive change.

The aftermath of 9/11 presented numerous opportunities for young people to lead and serve. Many did in ways that should be celebrated and replicated. But overall, as a group, young people missed the call of duty and another opportunity to live up to their promise as the "Next Greatest Generation."

Chapter 29

The 2002 Elections: Results, Proving Inaction

I wrote the following editorial shortly after the 2002 primary elections, which in Georgia took place one year and one day after the events of 9/11. The editorial is an admonishment about American inaction and a call for vigilance. I share it in the hopes that it serves as a reminder and wake-up call for participation. The text also sets the tone for the following section about "the Greatest Generation that never was" and their disengagement in the 2002 election. Sadly, the editorial has resonance today as well, considering so many citizens are not engaging on critical issues of education, the environment and the continuing quagmire in Iraq and what this all means to the long-term future of America and our world.

When "remembering" isn't enough
(Printed in the *Atlanta Journal Constitution* on 9.13.2002)

Americans paused this week to remember the tragic events of September 11, 2001. We stopped for a moment of silence and wore flags and pins in remembrance of the fallen heroes and victims of terrorism. Unfortunately, in this groundswell of sorrow and recollection, we neglect to see what and who America is today, September 11th, 2002.

If we closely scrutinize America one year later, we'd see a nation more patriotic, yet less engaged. A nation more concerned about global affairs, yet less active at the ballot box. As a result, our mourning is a hollow promise of civic action yet to come.

Abraham Lincoln's Gettysburg Address was quoted at readings from "Ground Zero" in New York City and in the Halls of Congress. The most poignant section of the speech tied the Civil War to today's memorials. In reference to consecrating the site of tragedy, Lincoln said, "...the brave men, living and dead, who struggled here have consecrated it, far above our poor power to add or detract."

Yet Lincoln left a call to action missed by most: "...That we here highly resolve that these dead shall not have died in vain — that this nation, under God, shall have a new birth of freedom — and that a government of the people, by the people, for the people, shall not perish from the earth," a real possibility today.

A critical indicator of America's health was buried in the September 11th news coverage. An election took place in Georgia this week and few people seemed to notice. Turnout was a shameful nine percent of eligible voters. While we remember those lost, we failed to take action in their name. The abysmal 26 percent participation in the Primary Election should deepen our concern.

Citizens do not see a connection between patriotism and civic action. The answers are visible if we merely stop to ask ourselves why. People are tired of partisanship and rhetoric, and want elected officials and candidates to focus on issues and voters. Because of this negativism, many people believe government is no longer "of the people," and has no relevance to their daily lives.

A recent Harvard study found that 60 percent of surveyed college students believe major problems are more likely to be solved through "volunteerism" than by "working with government." These students believe partisanship and special interests are drowning their voices and stalling government in its tracks.

Citizens also believe it is too difficult to get informed, and as a result, tune out. A recent study by the Community Foundation highlights the problem: Roughly 68 percent of Atlantans surveyed could not name one of their two U.S. Senators.

Elected officials see this inaction and ignore citizens who choose not to participate. Citizens that do not vote, voice concern over issues or provide campaign contributions, do not exist to our elected representatives. Can you blame legislators? They must make informed decisions on an array of issues, and do not have time to chase and engage citizens. As a result, debates of critical issues wither from the inattention of American citizens.

Hope does exist though. Americans are ready to be inspired and directed towards a common good. Citizens want to engage, but they need government to meet them half way. Change can happen, and people will act, if together, we discuss the issues affecting our daily lives.

And so, one year after September 11th, 2001, our world is an uncertain place, where people struggle to find work and make ends meet. Where terrorists lurk — both at home and abroad. Our schools are in need of repair and our environment cries out for industry and citizens to develop solutions irrespective of the political, jurisdictional or bottom lines.

Perhaps today, we should not quote Abraham Lincoln, but John F. Kennedy, who inspired a nation when he said, "The energy, the faith, the devotion which we bring to this endeavor will light our country and all who serve it — and the glow from that fire can truly light the world.

And so my fellow Americans: Ask not what your country can do for you — ask what you can do for your country."

Now is the time for us to reengage and reunite. Now we must make a solemn promise to get informed, build coalitions, get to know our elected officials and take action. These are the requirements of citizens that remember September 11ᵗʰ and decide to take charge of their own liberty.

The 2002 elections presented citizens with an opportunity to flex their political muscles following the tragic events of 9/11, and the close national election in 2000. Many experts hoped that the lessons gleaned from Election 2000 and the subsequent media tutorial would help people understand the significance of being involved — reversing the feeling of helplessness many felt at the ballot box. For young people, it presented another opportunity to define themselves and to take action.

Unfortunately, voters — young and older — missed the call of patriotism and basic civic duty. As outlined in the editorial at the start of this section, people stayed away from polling places across the country in droves. Here we were, one year removed from 9/11, with huge issues swirling about like going to war, shoring up Social Security and defending the homeland. It was a time when American voices needed to be heard. Voters should have been electing people they felt were most equipped to deal with the rising tide of issues. Instead, they stayed away from the polls en masse, in both the primary and general elections.

Turnout was particularly low during the primaries. In fact, turnout reached all-time lows in states that held both Democrat and Republican primaries. Participation in these states was actually more than 50 percent lower than in the late 1960s and early 1970s. Specifically, participation in the 16 states holding statewide primaries for both major parties averaged 16.2 percent of eligible voters, which is a decline from the 17.6 percent in 1998. The participation rate was down more than 51 percent from its peak turnout in 1966. Of the states with low turnout, nine set records, including Alabama, Arkansas, California, Iowa, Montana, Nebraska, New Mexico, Ohio and West Virginia.

An oft-reported reason for why young people and other disinterested citizens fail to participate is that they believe lobbyists and special interest groups dominate the political process. But the irony is, by participating at 9 percent in some states, citizens all but ensure that a small population of voters can disproportionately impact an election's outcome. It is a self-fulfilling prophecy.

The 2002 general elections reversed the decline in participation slightly and momentarily. Roughly 39 percent of the voting age population showed up at the polls, which was slightly higher than the 36 percent who came out in 1998, the last non-presidential election. Many experts attribute the increase in participation to some closely contested races and more organized grassroots outreach and get-out-the-vote drives, but not patriotism or duty.

Young people followed the overall voting trends in 2002. Slightly less than 20 percent of 18- to 24-year-olds voted, which was up minimally from the 18.5 percent who participated in 1998. But that still means that less than one in four young Americans bothered to cast a ballot.

According to a report by the Committee for the Study of the American Electorate, a non-partisan, nonprofit research organization, turnout increased in 31 states, but dropped in 19 and the District of Columbia. Seven states set record lows for voter participation in an off-year election and only Florida established a record high. A close examination of election data shows that states experiencing the largest increases in voter turnout were places where there were high-profile, hotly contested elections.

As a result of these close contests, political parties, special interest groups and candidates put record amounts of money and human capital into these races. Of particular note was organizational and campaign focuses on grassroots outreach and get-out-the-vote activities. This is an important point that will be examined further in the final sections of this book. Organized efforts to mobilize people work when voters see an opportunity to make a difference in the outcome of an election. Voters go to the polls when issues are hotly debated or have particular meaning to their daily lives.

It is a positive sign of American engagement that minor increases in voter turnout took place during the 2002 General Election. However, more than 60 percent of Americans typically fail to vote in midterm contests and nearly half of all eligible voters stay on the sidelines during presidential elections. And the 2002 elections failed to produce the type of turnout that would have signaled the awakening of a generation. Young people continued to be disengaged in the electoral process even though so much was transpiring in the world around them. And the trend of tepid participation has continued the past several off-year elections. Turnout of voting-aged citizens was only 41 percent in 2006, a 1 percent rise from 2002.

Chapter 30

Conclusion

Traditionally, a generation becomes more civically and politically active over time as personal and professional responsibilities mount, which increases interaction with government at all levels. The older we get, the more we encounter taxes and other issues that make us aware of government's presence. So while it is possible that this generation will track with the actions of previous ones, it is not a guarantee, and few trend-altering activities loom on the horizon.

Many experts predicted that seismic world or political events like those experienced in the past few years could jump start the current generation of young people, leading to the next Greatest Generation. Perhaps on some levels it is too early to judge young people on the role they will play in the future success or failure of American democracy. As previously outlined, the immediate aftermath of Election 2000 and the events of 9/11 produced minimal new civic activity among America's young people.

By contrast, Election 2004 witnessed a degree of increased activity. MTV's Choose or Lose campaigns and other significant mobilization efforts for this election helped to increase turnout among voters

30 years old, or younger. Early results show that more than 21 million young people went to the polls in 2004. That's up from about 16 million in 2000 when roughly 42 percent of the generation went to the polls.

There seemed to be a rising sense among Americans young and old that the 2004 elections were extremely important — something they had to participate in. The election was closely contested and people believed their voice could be heard and their vote counted. The lessons of 2000 seemed to be sinking in, bringing people to the polls in record numbers.

Unfortunately, the 2006 elections prove we haven't made vast progress. The election was another opportunity for significant change, and it seemed Americans were wrapped up in the contest. Yet turnout was a mere 41 percent. We should note that the trend of declining participation has halted and we've seen slight up-ticks the past few years. This could be the point where long-term change has begun, but it's just too early to tell!

However, regardless of the slight rise from year-to-year, we must ask why nearly half of all young Americans stayed home on Election Day. Why, at a time with so much at stake, were they willing to remain on the sidelines? Turnout was up, yet even after the 2000 election, events of September 11 and significant outreach by both political parties, MTV and programs like P. Diddy's "Vote or Die," half of America's young people remained disengaged. This begs the question, what, if anything can change the attitudes and long-term behavior of America's youth?

Something has to give, because no cohort of young people in the last 40 years has begun with such minimal levels of interest or activity in politics and the civic process. Young people seem to be tuning out, rather than turning out, en masse. A 2000 survey by the National Election Studies organization found that 40 percent of Generation X and Y respondents had not watched a national news broadcast on TV in the past week and 35 percent said they did not read a newspaper in the same timeframe. Surely, some of these respondents were getting their news from an alternate source, like the Internet. Yet, it is difficult to effectively engage in the civic process if uninformed about the events taking place in local communities, across the nation and around the world.

Today's generations of young people — X and Y — were presented with numerous opportunities to rise to the occasion of civic leadership and participation in the immediate wake of Election 2000 and the events of September 11. This was their opportunity to follow the example set by their grandparents and great-grandparents, becoming a guiding force of action in America. Unfortunately, on average, these generations are missing their chance and remain a prospect of leadership, apparently still waiting for that cause that will unite and rally them.

The life experiences of Generations X and Y to date have made them more skeptical of government and their fellow citizens, leading to a perception that government has little meaning to their daily lives. This is a scary prospect for America's future unless we can find ways to reverse the trend. While not a rosy conclusion, there is hope. As this book has pointed out time and again, people will engage when they see connections between government and their daily lives, when elections are closely contested and when candidates engage with them, not talking over them.

Young people, the least active group in America, need special attention if we are to engage more than only half of them in the civic process. Ask employers in this new age of hiring if they have had to alter the approach to employee compensation and retention. The answer would be a resounding, "yes." These new generations see the world very differently and require different methods of engagement.

An important first step to rebuilding a generation of civic leaders begins in the home, as most good lessons should. Parents need to discuss politics and world events with their children. And they should take them to the polls on Election Day. Our schools and community groups have a critical role to play as well. They must do a better job of including civic lessons in all of their activities. The lessons must be introduced at the start of schooling, in kindergarten, and reinforced through high school and college.

The final section of this book examines several case studies of successfully engaging people in the civic process. Combined with the lessons just outlined, we can build upon the results of Election 2004 to engage more young people (and all Americans) in the civic process. It is a monumental challenge, but one that must be undertaken if we are to ensure Abraham Lincoln's vision: "A government of the people, by the people, for the people."

Section VI

Chapters 31 – 36

Rebuilding Civic Participation:
Lessons From the Trenches.

Chapter 31

Introduction

Much of this book has been dedicated to enumerating the deficits in American civic participation, offering dire predictions for the future if current habits aren't altered. While somewhat negative in tone, the preceding chapters were necessary to provide a clear understanding of civic history and the reasons for our current state of affairs. We can now move forward to celebrate and rejuvenate pride in American civic duty. If the previous sections provided a critical look at our past and present, this section highlights tools to brighten and secure our future.

For all the heralded failures and negatives associated with our recent civic experiment, there are thousands of successful attempts to mobilize people that should be celebrated and emulated. I have been fortunate enough to participate in a number of civic initiatives that provided firsthand knowledge about why being involved matters. These experiences also provide insight into what will ultimately move citizens to action.

The experiences include: working in government as a legislative aide in the Georgia Secretary of State's office; pounding the campaign trail as a political press secretary; shaping public policy at a grassroots level; engaging people through nonprofit programming; and managing media and community relations across the Southeast for the No. 1 company on *Fortune Magazines* 2007 list of American companies. Each position afforded me an opportunity to engage people of all ages, races, education and socio-economic levels to find out what issues mattered to them and to gauge their opinions on government and elected officials.

These experiences also allowed me to travel a good bit, giving talks to churches, schools and nonprofits, while also rolling up my sleeves to assist with community service projects. While there always seemed to be some pessimism regarding the civic process, people at each stop wanted to be involved. They had issues that kept them awake at night, like their children's education, the health of our environment or other concerns ranging from taxation to individual freedoms and rights.

But regardless of the issue — or of how frustrated people were with the system — they cared enough to show up and make their voices heard. They were there to learn, make connections with others and take action. But the most striking element of these experiences was the passion with which people voiced their position. For all the naysayers who point to our dwindling levels of participation, I encourage them to visit a school board meeting, a community town hall or a local forum about zoning for a new Wal-Mart store. People show up to each because they care and want to be heard. The case studies that follow provide evidence as to why each experience emboldened and inspired me to teach others the tools for civic action, while helping them find their voice in the process.

No matter what the problem, someone will inevitably say, "no silver bullet exists to solve it." In general, that's a true statement. Most problems facing our communities cannot be solved by one simple answer or solution. However, my experiences in the trenches show that one powerful tool does exist for engaging people in the civic process: making the issues relevant to peoples' daily lives — making it personal.

Obviously, the complexity of issues facing us today makes this seem like a relatively naïve statement. But when issues and government are made real and relevant for people, they take notice because they have skin in the game. And people are more likely to get informed and take action when the issues being debated have tangible outcomes. This section of the book examines real world case studies of programs and campaigns that moved people to action. The lessons gleaned from each experience provide tools for shaping our nation's future, even if the examples are local in nature.

The simple and powerful truth is that people will engage. But they need to be invited into the civic process, inspired to action and convinced their voices will be heard along the way.

Chapter 32

The Clean Water Initiative: Public Education and Building Consensus for the Common Good

A significant barrier to civic participation in this country is the belief that government is beholden to special interests and not the people. This bias prevents positive policy solutions that improve the lives of everyday citizens. While this isn't the central reason, policy solutions at all levels of government fail, or are less effective because they are held hostage to stakeholder needs and viewpoints that are too wildly divergent.

This is particularly true of environmental issues at all levels of government and in all parts of our nation. Government institutions must balance the needs of its people, which often forces them to become referees between big business, the community and conservationists. Elected officials and bureaucrats must create rules that protect our limited natural resources, while providing businesses with access to the elements that allow them to meet public demand for their products.

Care and use of America's waterways is one of the most frequent and passionate debates in the various halls of government these days. Water is a finite resource that nourishes our crops, makes our communities green and vibrant, and is a vital part of countless processes in our world — including human sustenance. As such, its use is constantly examined and debated. Communities around America are being forced to discuss this issue more than ever as our nation grows and consumes more water for all aspects of life and, as is the current case in the Southeast, drought sucks our water supplies dry.

Atlanta is no exception and in recent years has become a poster child for mismanagement of its limited water resources. The city is a national success story on many levels: a population that has doubled since 1970; four of the nation's 10 fastest growing counties; and an economy that continues to outpace other regions nationwide. Of course, this unparalleled growth also brings negative byproducts to the region.

For instance, it's no secret across the nation that Atlanta suffers from horrendous traffic, poor air quality and other growth issues. But until recently, it wasn't widely known that a serious water quality problem exists. Few people understood that, as a by-product of regional success, more than 1,000 miles of impaired streams and rivers are reaching their capacity to accept wastewater discharges. A 2000 federal lawsuit was forcing the region to evaluate the severity of the situation and resolve the issue on an accelerated schedule, one of the most stringent in the nation.

Atlanta, like most large American urban cores, is more than just a "city." It is a collection of towns, cities and county governments that make up a Metropolitan Statistical Area (MSA). As a result, "Atlanta's" problems are actually DeKalb County's problems. They are also Snellville's problems and Roswell's problems, etc. In other words, the issues faced by metro Atlanta and other growing MSA's, are actually *regional issues, requiring regional solutions.* But too often, parochial agendas, concerns over spending and sharing local government dollars have precluded solutions that truly bring about positive and long-term results.

That's why the Metro Atlanta Chamber of Commerce and the Regional Business Coalition created the Clean Water Initiative (CWI) Task Force in 2000. It was a committee of business, conservation and government leaders tasked with developing solutions to metro Atlanta's storm water runoff and wastewater management problems. And as mentioned above, these three interest groups often have differing opinions on the use and protection of natural resources. So it was the committee's job to reach a decision that went beyond jurisdictional, political and bottom lines to solve the region's growing water crisis. No small task, somewhat akin to herding wild cats.

Several months before the CWI Task Force began, the League of Conservation Voters conducted a poll, which found that Georgia voters were very concerned about both air and water quality issues — only education and crime/drugs drew slightly higher concern ratings. Yet the majority of people were unaware of solutions that could solve Atlanta's water problems. Nor were they confident that government could create or implement the solutions. The poll numbers seemed to be reinforced by a history of mistrust and apprehension among committee members — limiting the likelihood that a solution would be found.

And so, the Task Force commenced a six-month journey to learn more about the region's water problems and what systems and solutions had been implemented in other parts of the world to address similar local water issues. A few factors combined to make Atlanta's situation particularly unique: it is the largest city in the world supplied by such a small body of water; the state has 159 counties; and there was extreme court pressure to establish plans for solving the region's water woes. Only about 10 percent of the state's waters had been tested by the Environmental Protection Division at the time of the Task Force's creation, and more than 1,000 miles of rivers and streams in the region already failed to meet water quality standards.

Storm water runoff pollutants contributed to approximately 85 percent of the water quality violations. This type of runoff has an almost immeasurable number of sources on land and is essentially uncontrolled, unlike municipal or industrial facility discharges that are generally "permitted" by government agencies. Storm water runoff is rain that falls on the land, washing pollutants into rivers and streams. This pollution includes petroleum residue from roads and parking lots, fertilizers and pesticides from yards, and sediment and heavy metals from disturbed land and construction sites. In essence, the Chattahoochee River (Atlanta's main water source) and other rivers in the region are "full" because of both wastewater and storm water runoff.

If the environmental challenges were not enough for the committee to consider, federal court orders required that the region develop Total Maximum Daily Loads (TMDLs) by 2004 for each type of pollutant making its way into every Georgia waterway that didn't meet the prescribed quality standards. The court orders complicated matters for Task Force members — any solution would require better controls of storm water runoff because the simple elimination of pollutants being controlled by wastewater treatment plants would not achieve compliance with the TMDLs.

In very real terms, any Task Force recommendation required controls on how we built homes and commercial properties, how we cared for our lawns and other aspects of daily life that contribute to runoff. Growth and prosperity could be diminished by a moratorium on building permits if the Task Force failed and the region didn't develop plans to reduce the pollution. There was a very real threat that

Georgia's economic engine — Atlanta — could be shut down! Some of these fears are being realized now as entire industries (car washes, nurseries, landscaping companies, etc.) succumb to the drought raging across the southeast.

So the Task Force was under a great deal of pressure when it held regular meetings to analyze the region's current problems and review best practices used in other major metropolitan areas. The education process was the easy part. Committee members learned the seriousness of the region's problems and what would happen if no special actions were taken. At a minimum, astronomical budget allocations would be necessary to repair the crumbling sewer infrastructure and to build new treatment plants (the resulting price tag for the project was estimated at $3 billion dollars for the City of Atlanta, alone). The negative consequences also could include sewer tap moratoriums, which would end construction because no new building could "tap into" the regions water grid. And the federal government could step in and take control of local water management.

The true challenge was getting Task Force members to work together — moving beyond their own special interests towards a solution that would have a positive effect for the entire region. You'd think that a problem this severe would lead people to put aside their personal, political or professional interests for the good of the whole. Unfortunately, it wasn't that easy. As we know, Americans are not very good at taking the longview of problems facing us — just ask Al Gore about his long fight to get people's attention regarding global warming.

Elected officials on the committee were supposedly representing "the people," meaning they had to keep their constituents' best interests in mind. While clean water is a necessity, so is the prudent expenditure of tax dollars and political capital. And so, many of the Task Force members representing cities, counties and towns outside the city of Atlanta were reluctant to help fund a solution to the region's water problems since they "didn't create them in the first place" and have almost no jurisdiction over the pipes and sewers within the city limits. On the flipside, city of Atlanta leaders felt they shouldn't be responsible for the bulk of the solutions either, as only roughly 400,000 of metro Atlanta's five million people live within the city limits. Task Force representatives from the city of Atlanta argued that this was a region-wide problem requiring truly regional participation.

Business leaders were concerned that resulting regulations or protocols would elevate the cost of production to the point where running a business or developing affordable residential and commercial buildings would be impossible. It was feared that increased production charges would elevate rent, housing costs and other measures, eliminating Atlanta's competitive advantage against similar cities across America. This is a simplification of the argument to be sure. But the key point is that the business community's needs were, on some level, in conflict with potential Task Force recommendations.

And finally, representatives from the conservation community believed not enough had been done in the past to protect the environment. There seemed to be a real sense that many of the proposals being discussed were not strict enough for conservation leaders' tastes. Task Force members from the business community were angling for far less oversight than the conservationists, who wanted strict monitoring and enforcement.

The best public policy often falls "in the middle" because it represents a compromise between multiple viewpoints. With compromise, neither party gets everything they asked for in the negotiation. But each side ends up with some of their desired outcomes and is more likely to outwardly support the resulting policy. In too many environmental debates, business leaders have either opposed any action or offered counter-proposals their opponents considered untenable. By the same token, too many groups in the environmental movement have been unwilling to yield even a little to achieve some gains for the environment. The old line "a good plan today is better than the perfect plan never" rings true in these instances. In many debates, conservationists have missed an opportunity for even minor improvements because of their unwillingness to compromise just a little.

But to the conservationist community's credit, a number of the gains in clean air, better water and other environmental initiatives would not have been achieved without the "line in the sand attitude" brought to the table during the debate. Nevertheless, one is left wondering how the relations between "adversaries" might differ if a greater atmosphere of trust and compromise existed on both sides of the ongoing environmental debate. What else could have been accomplished if a more open dialogue calling for a common sense approach to public policy existed among parties?

It took the leadership of representatives from all Task Force "camps" to foster the development of consensus and public policy with a viable chance of achieving positive results. The participants understood that potentially, the literal future of the region hung in the balance. Without reform, the courts would enforce sewer tap moratoriums limiting or halting new construction. And the courts could have taken over some parts of Atlanta city government to ensure changes were made to existing water management policies and practices. These actions would impact tax rates, downgrade Atlanta's bond valuation and ultimately diminish growth as businesses and people would relocate to more economically stable areas. Potential economic collapse for the city of Atlanta wasn't in any group's best interests.

The downward spiral would have continued as the existence of fewer businesses and homes would reduce local government's tax base — limiting their ability to provide basic services to their citizens. And in turn, a diminished tax base would provide fewer resources for government to protect our environment — a risky proposition for the conservationists at the table. Sewer moratoriums and draconian government regulations would prevent businesses from growing and boosting profits. A declining national image would limit relocation of companies, which diminishes growth of the economy at large. The conservationists realized that being involved in the process and creating manageable solutions would serve the dual purpose of improving the region's waters and creating an environment for increased future supervision and regulation.

Each party involved understood that their self-interest was latched to the best interests of the region. And after extensively studying a range of best practices, the Task Force completed recommendations in October of 2000 and delivered them to state and local elected officials in January of 2001. The new entity proposed by the group would be charged with studying water use, abuse and future needs. And they would have the additional authority to craft a regional water management plan and enforce moderate repercussions for violations. Their work is still really getting underway, so it's too early to quantify their impact.

In the end, the Georgia General Assembly adopted approximately 95 percent of the Task Force's recommendations, creating the Metropolitan North Georgia Water Planning District, which was signed into law by Governor Roy Barnes in July 2001. No party walked away from the table 100 percent happy, and there were certainly contentious debates. But the "best plan never" was replaced with a "good plan today" that will have tangible, although incremental, positive results.

And through the process, the general public learned about the problem in greater detail and became more willing to do their part to change the current state of affairs. The Metro Atlanta Chamber of Commerce commissioned a second poll when the Task Force completed its work. The same baseline questions and the same pollster were used to gauge public attitudes following nearly six months of community education on the issue. The new poll, conducted in October of 2000, found essentially the same high levels of awareness about the problem but indicated that concern over water quality was now higher than Atlanta's much more visible air quality problems. Further, the research found that a majority of Georgians agreed with a central Task Force recommendation that local governments should be "required" to work across city and county lines to solve water quality issues.

The poll included a question designed to gauge voters' willingness to pay for the multi-billion dollar long-term cost of dealing with the area's water quality problems, a central focus of the Task Force's work. An astonishing 75 percent of respondents expressed a willingness to pay at least $1 to $5 per month in new taxes devoted to water quality. So it wasn't just the Task Force participants who learned through the process. Local citizens also became educated about the critical nature of the situation and saw their stake in the solution. **There is a powerful lesson from this case study: positive change is possible when people understand the importance of the issue, have a stake in the process and feel beholden to something larger than their own self-interest in finding a solution.**

Chapter **33**

Vote for America: Making the Civic Process Relevant

The previous chapter showed us that people take action when they feel informed about critical issues, see themselves as part of a larger whole and understand that their actions have real implications for change. In this section, the problem of civic inactivity will be tackled by making government relevant to people's daily lives. Examining the activities of Vote for America will allow us to see what happens when people realize they have a personal stake in the process and understand the importance of taking action to make their voices count.

Matt Brown founded Vote for America (VFA) in 2000 as a way to improve educated voter turnout in the state of Rhode Island. The organization recruited thousands of volunteers and is given significant credit for the state's 5.6 percent increase in voter turnout the same year — more than a 41 percent jump among young voters. It is difficult to accurately quantify a program's direct impact on voter turnout; however, a review of the facts provides compelling evidence about VFA's impact. The VFA effort was the only major voter program taking place in the state that year. And neither major presidential candidate made an appearance in Rhode Island or ran a single campaign ad. So it's not hard to give credit to this organization for being at least partly responsible for the increased voter turnout, especially considering very few external forces were driving civic awareness and participation.

The VFA founders realized that "politics as usual" wasn't capturing America's attention as evidenced by Election 2000, where half of all eligible American voters chose not to participate. So they created a unique, nonpartisan organization that attempted to strengthen democracy by asking citizens from all walks of life and political backgrounds to commit to voting through Pledge to Vote Drives. The program is genius in its simplicity.

The voter drives were built with a "Democracy Pyramid:" volunteers recruited friends, neighbors and co-workers who pledged to be informed and thoughtful voters and provided them with the information — free of partisan rhetoric — necessary to accomplish this task. Community leaders formed a Steering Committee "at the top" of the pyramid that secured influential people to serve as Democracy Fellows. These Fellows recruited volunteers or Democracy Captains, who secured pledges to vote within their community and provided program guidance throughout the campaign. And finally, the Captains secured a certain number of pledged voters and provided them with information about why voting matters, delivered nonpartisan information about candidates and the voting process, and ensured they got to the polls on Election Day. It's essentially a pyramid scheme, but for positive civic gains.

Rebecca Lieberman, daughter of Senator Joe Lieberman (I-CT), took over the program with an eye towards moving VFA nationwide. In 2001, they used the Democracy Pyramid approach in New York City to educate voters about changes to the primary elections following the events of September 11. That fateful morning was actually a primary voting day in New York. Many voters had gone to the polls in the morning, prior to the attacks, so there was a great deal of confusion around when they would be rescheduled and who would be allowed to vote. Vote for America built a Democracy Pyramid to inform voters of the changes, which contributed to the largest primary turnout in more than a decade. Rebecca developed a blue print for taking the program nationwide, which included expanding into North Carolina and Georgia for the 2002 off-year elections.

She selected me to lead the effort in Georgia, which sought to recruit thousands of new voters in the 11-county metro Atlanta area, including Athens-Clarke County, home of the University of Georgia. I was running a public affairs firm and nonprofit — Coalition for a Voting America — at the time (more on that to come). So this new role was a natural fit. My first task was to secure the Steering Committee members who would be responsible for providing credibility and funds, and recruiting volunteers. We recruited 72 Steering Committee participants who represented both the public and private sectors, academia, elected officials, community groups and people of all political persuasions.

Vote for America-Georgia (VFA-GA) ultimately recruited more than 500 volunteers and secured nearly 2,000 Pledge to Vote Cards, which were used to confirm new voters. Georgians ignored rain and other election barriers to defy a national trend of declining voter participation in midterm elections, increasing turnout from about 46.2 percent of registered voters in 1998 to roughly 54.2 percent in 2002. The program worked because it empowered people from all walks of life to talk to their friends, family and co-workers about the issues and candidates on the ballot and the importance of being thoughtful voters. The 2002 elections were particularly partisan. And candidates discussed issues or proposals rather limitedly, relying instead on negative tactics such as attacks on past voting records and personal character and integrity. These factors generally tend to suppress voter turnout. That's why in at least a small part, VFA-GA and its volunteers' focus on issues and voters, not rhetoric and partisanship, is widely-credited with helping to bring people into the process.

VFA-GA measured first-year success in two ways: total number of volunteers and pledged voters recruited; and the ability to elevate discussions of elections through media and personal outreach. The staff worked tirelessly to get the program's message out and to implore people to take part in their communities. More than 10 million individual "impressions" were made through these efforts, which included presentations at church services, after school programs, Kiwanis and Rotary meetings, college organizations and corporate training seminars. The staff also worked extensively with the media, earning an additional 44 million individual impressions through television, radio, newspaper and online stories. Vote for America volunteers used kneecap-to-kneecap conversations and fun events like "Grilling for America" to encourage people to take the pledge to be educated voters.

As mentioned earlier, VFA-GA initially set a lofty goal of recruiting thousands of pledged voters in metro Atlanta and Athens for the 2002 Election. It became evident as the program rolled on that this would be an enormous challenge and was not really the only true measure of success (especially considering the staff of four got to work a mere five months before the election). It became clear that volunteer trainings, dissemination of the Democracy Toolkit, "get out the vote" week activities (election-week activities designed to encourage participation) and new voter machine education were meaningful ways of elevating the awareness of, and participation in elections. So the program can surely be called a success even though it did not reach the initial voter recruitment goal.

Implementing the Democracy Pyramid and working face-to-face with citizens — engaging many of them for the first time — gave VFA staff insight into why voter turnout had continued to decline almost every election since 1964. The 2002 election proved beyond a shadow of a doubt that people want candidates to engage them in discussions of issues and the civic process instead of simply relying on fundraising-driven TV advertising to reach them. Elected officials should pay attention, because voters across America sent them a clear message: "Ignore us and engage in negative attacks instead of substantive discussions of issues, and we'll boot you at the ballot box."

The most poignant lesson taken from the Vote for America campaign is that people participate when the process is made relevant to their daily lives. Countless stories could bring this point home, but the most inspiring took place at the University of Georgia (UGA). I was giving a speech on campus in Athens, trying to recruit new volunteers to the program. Students were politely interested, but it was clear that they were probably there more to be with friends or for the free food than to seriously engage in the program.

However, we signed up nearly every student in the room because we made voting meaningful to their daily lives by showing how government goes about its business with or without them. It became clear to audience members that legislation happens. It's just a question of whether it happens with them or to them!

The hook used that night to awaken college students to the process was fairly obvious. The Georgia General Assembly became a national leader in education financing — pre-K and college — when it launched the Hope Scholarship in 1992. Through the program, every graduating high school senior that earns a minimum B average receives full tuition grants to any Georgia institution of higher learning. The students must maintain a B average once there, to continue receiving free tuition, room and board and book stipends. All in all, it's a good deal and has gone a long way toward improving the state's higher education system because it keeps the most talented students from going to schools outside of Georgia.

The Hope Scholarship is a tremendous benefit that a significant number of UGA students enjoy. I used this issue to bring home the point that being involved in the civic process is important to each college student's daily life. Georgia was still running a budget surplus in 2002, thanks to one of the fastest growing economies in the Southeast (and the nation). Yet there was a very real possibility that the state, like most others around the nation, would begin feeling the effects of the sour economy.

I first asked the audience to raise their hand if they were attending UGA on the Hope Scholarship. As expected, nearly all the hands in the room shot up. I next asked students what they would do if an elected official introduced legislation to use Hope funds, which are completely generated by the state's lottery, to secure a faltering budget. I detailed a scenario where an elected official responded to projected budget short-falls by raiding Hope to pay for the state's booming Medicare program, prison expansion or an array of other budget needs. Many students sat with a panicked look on their face — a cross between disbelief that the scenario was possible and uncertainty of what they would do to fight the legislation. Perhaps the most unique response was that the students didn't need to do anything — "our parents pay the bills and they vote, so elected officials will listen to them." I really couldn't argue with the logic, but was taken aback by the complexity of the argument for why, even in the most-dire of personal situations for a student, voting didn't matter.

We discussed the issue a bit longer and it became clear to students that taking action was the best way to save their scholarships. Leaving the "fight" in the hands of other people was too risky a proposition. And so, nearly every student in the room that evening signed up to take part in the Pledge to Vote Drive. Some of VFA-GA's greatest successes in 2002 can be traced back to Athens and the students at UGA. This is because in large part, the VFA staff and student volunteers were able to convince their peers that being involved in the civic process has a direct bearing on their daily life. We weren't offering prizes, perks or other incentives for people to get involved and turn out to the polls. It's simply that the message sunk in: *legislation happens. It's just a question of whether it happens to you or with you.* And voting and being engaged in the civic process is critical in holding elected officials accountable and to solve issues that matter to each of us.

Chapter 34

Coalition for a Voting America: Providing the Tools of Participation

People give many reasons for their decision not to participate in the American civic process. As was well-chronicled throughout the book, the reasons range from feelings of helplessness and distrust to being turned off by partisan rhetoric and the lack of progress on major issues. But if you stop for a moment to talk with people face-to-face about their decision, many will say they simply don't know how to get informed or become active. Years of research and numerous conversations at programs and speeches made clear that a lack of basic civic tools was a significant barrier to participation.

And so, that's why a major focus of the Coalition for a Voting America (CVA) was arming people with basic information they could use about how government worked and ways citizens could take meaningful action. We believed that education and empowerment were major keys to unlocking a flood of civic enthusiasm and participation. In this section, we'll examine what happens when you empower people with the tools of democracy by analyzing some real world encounters from the Coalition for a Voting America.

Seeds for the Coalition for a Voting America were sewn during graduate school when I examined the youth voter mobilization efforts of groups like Rock the Vote and MTV Choose or Lose — outlined previously. The research allowed me to see what successfully mobilized young people to civic action and what did not. Unfortunately, making money and repaying student loans was a personal priority upon leaving graduate school. And having just completed a tour of duty as campaign press secretary for Mark Taylor, who was elected Lieutenant Governor of Georgia in 1998, earning a paycheck took top priority. As a result, plans for launching an organization to address America's growing civic divide were shelved.

Instead, I went to work for a public relations agency, getting a taste of issue management like the Clean Water Initiative outlined in the first chapter in this section. But the passion for making a difference never dissipated. In fact, it grew after engaging people around the Kyoto Protocol, health care concerns and several other issues being debated under the "Gold Dome" of Georgia's General Assembly and across the nation. Yet making the leap into the nonprofit world still seemed ill-timed. And perhaps more importantly, the best way to make a difference in the lives of people looking to engage in the civic process still eluded me. That is, until my very own "Jerry Maguire" moment took place.

I was reading *The Buying of the President 2000* by Charles Lewis and the Center for Public Integrity one morning around 2 a.m.,, in the summer of 1999. At the end of this book about campaign finance reform, the author proclaimed that democracy could be lost to the influence of special interest groups in the 2000 election if immediate reforms were not implemented. The author hoped that reform would truly bring about President Abraham Lincoln's vision of a government, "of the people, by the people, and for the people."

And voila! The light bulb lit up, and I literally jumped out of bed, turned on the computer and began writing a "mission statement." The document generated that night was the foundation for CVA's business plan. In the movie, Jerry succumbed to bad pizza, which generated his new vision. My excuse is the evident lack of a social life that had me reading about campaign finance reform for fun during the wee hours of a Wednesday morning!

It took a few months to finish the model and to get buy-in from key supporters. But we finalized plans and produced a living document to guide our efforts. I left my PR firm, picked up some individual clients and began moving forward recruiting funding and board members for CVA.

As outlined in the plan, "The Coalition for a Voting America was a non-partisan public interest group leading a call to civic action. By identifying barriers to civic participation, educating communities at the grassroots level about the importance of making our voices heard, and proposing effective reforms to enable meaningful participation in the processes of government, CVA is lighting the fire of civic passion across the boundaries of age, race, and economic status — because we share the belief: We the people can govern."

Coalition for a Voting America was a new organization, and the problem of low civic participation had been around for decades. So small but meaningful steps were the order of the day in our fight to reverse diminishing participation. Showing early successes was the only way CVA would gain support and credibility. We couldn't set out to change the world overnight. Instead, CVA needed to attack the problem one program and one citizen at a time.

We created a handful of programs that effectively attacked diminishing civic and electoral participation in a comprehensive manner. Together, with a coalition of volunteers, organizations and grassroots leaders, we attempted to implement the following programs:

The Liberty Action Academy: a grassroots program similar to voter education schools during the Civil Rights Movement where teams of facilitators worked with local community groups (churches, neighborhood associations, etc.) and provided the tools necessary to educate and activate their members and constituents — "teaching the teachers." Topics for the Liberty Action Academy model included voter registration, media training, coalition building, starting Civic Roundtables, and teaching *Talking to Our Government*, a CVA publication included on our current website (www.michaelpmills.biz).

A group of Emory University students served as our pilot for this program. We first tested their knowledge of the civic process and their interest in becoming civic mentors in their community. The student group's efforts culminated with a Civic Roundtable (discussed next) of campus issues. The group was able to turn out an enthusiastic bunch of students who held a lively debate about solutions to local campus issues, including the lack of campus media focus on student elections. This one program reinforced some points made in previous chapters: students do want to engage in the process, as they did in this roundtable, but the issues must be relevant to their daily lives, and they must feel like a resolution is possible — *that they have the voice and power to make a difference.*

We initially recommended that the group hold their roundtable on local transportation issues since a community debate was raging about whether to expand MARTA, Atlanta's subway system, to campus and through nearby residential neighborhoods. We hoped the transportation forum would provide an opportunity for students and community residents to dialogue about a critical issue for both "communities." Unfortunately, program organizers were fearful that students would lose control of the debate to the "experts" and their neighbors — forgetting for a moment that they reside in that community and have just as much right to voice an opinion as the homeowners did.

While the Liberty Action Academy was a limited experiment, the experience of trying to coax young people into taking the lead on such an important issue lent credence to the notion that students will participate when given the tools to make a difference. But they must feel like they possess the power to be heard. Otherwise, they turn inward toward issues they can control and influence, which oftentimes means we lose an important perspective in critical debates.

The Civic Roundtable: a monthly community meeting that provided citizens with a roadmap to the civic process, educated them about critical issues and spurred them to action. Elected officials, community activists and civic leaders discussed issues directly with the audience, who committed to action on the topics discussed. The "action" took various forms across the civic continuum, including letters to the editor, meetings with elected officials and hosting additional, educational community gatherings. Next to *Talking to Our Government*, the Civic Roundtable was CVA's most successful program.

The premise is simple: convene a group of interested citizens to learn and talk about critical issues of local, national or global import and culminate with an action item that ensures future participation. A panel of elected officials and experts from multiple sides of an issue were recruited to openly discuss their take on the matter at hand. Each panelist made his or her case to the audience in a five- to 10-minute introduction. The panel would then face questions from the moderator and audience, hoping to develop a broad discussion of the topic. The audience would then be split into small "roundtables" once the issue had been thoroughly discussed as a group.

The small group discussions were truly the magic of the program. All participants introduced themselves to the others at their table, explained why they attended the event, where they lived and gave their opinion (if they were comfortable doing so) on the issue discussed.

Someone from each of the small "roundtables" was responsible for providing a brief re-cap for the entire group when the discussions ended. Each group was also encouraged to discuss any other issues they felt needed attention in their communities. But more importantly, each participant had to announce to the group one civic activity he or she would complete in the next few months in response to the discussion. Announcing where each participant lived was important because this allowed for the creation of alliances and coalitions if people lived in the same community and felt passionately about the same issue.

The entire group would reconvene to review the individual roundtable discussions. The moderator then wrapped up the event and passed out a postcard-sized index card that each audience member was required to fill out. Participants wrote their civic action on one side and their address on the other. CVA mailed the card to them in 30 days as a reminder, an accountability check to complete the stated activity.

Roundtables covered a range of topics, including water quality, traffic, America's response to the terrorist attacks of 9/11 and election issues. Each program provided a new lesson about engaging people in the civic process. The Civic Roundtables worked because they educated people about issues, broke down the barriers to elected officials by engaging both sides in substantive discussions and provided tangible and basic actions that participants could take to embark on their civic journey.

Talking to Our Government: is a civic primer with basic information about how government works; rules for interacting with various branches of local, state or federal bureaucracy; and tools for taking action. The information was accessible so that people of all levels of civic understanding could walk away better informed, without being discouraged or embarrassed to ask basic questions. The document was available online and was also distributed at speaking engagements, roundtables and other events.

Talking to our Government was well-received because of its clear, basic and non-jargon driven approach to detailing the civic process. It outlined the basic rights and benefits associated with citizenship. But the booklet also stressed the responsibilities for interacting with government. In the end, *Talking to Our Government* was a success because it was accessible and humanized the civic process, reinforcing the message that people from all races, religions, classes and education levels need more information on how government works. As a nation, we fail to teach citizens enough about the process and do not engender a sense of civic participation at an early age, nor do we reinforce it throughout life. This document provided that missing context for people.

Chapter 35

Conclusion

Working on the front lines of the civic process has been reward-ing on multiple levels. Seeing the look of recognition in people's eyes that says they know it's possible to make a difference after becoming empowered and informed is priceless and heartening. The first half of this book revealed a nation slipping into a civic coma. While the stats of our civic decline are sobering, they are not the death knell of a once mighty nation.

Instead, seeing people turn on to the process once empowered, en-gaged, respected and educated proves that we can solve this problem. It makes clear that America's pulse is beating strong, although perhaps quietly. We must ensure that people have a fundamental understand-ing of the rights and responsibilities of citizenship, are equipped with the tools for successful action and are invited into the process.

Hopefully this section of the book inspired you to make a change in your world and got you primed for action. The following section will teach the basic tools for active citizenship. Read on and let the journey begin!

Chapter 36

Civic Participation Will Flourish — When Americans Take Part

Hopefully this book told the story of America at a crossroads. While it pointed to a number of negative indicators of American civic health, it also spotlighted significantly increasing levels of volunteerism and incremental rises in voter turnout. There are also a number of positive lessons in the case studies just discussed that prove this problem of declining participation can be solved if we instill a sense of civic responsibility in our communities and work together to understand the issues and build accountability for participating.

The United States is a place of great opportunity, diversity, tolerance, hope and prosperity. The nation was built by our Founding Fathers, who created an amazing document and core principles that guide our daily lives more than 225 years later. It is also built on a strong foundation of civic leadership laid by the Greatest Generation who showed the importance of sacrifice, commitment, integrity and action.

Yet today, the nation is divided politically, along issues of morality and purpose. In the last few years, Americans have endured tremendous hardship and political uncertainty, from Election 2000 and a sour economy to the events of 9/11. The resulting raw emotion piled onto a national cynicism and apathy that was built over decades because of events like Vietnam, Watergate, Iran Contra and the scandals of the Clinton years. The divisiveness continues as a Democratically-controlled Congress battles with President Bush over immigration reform, the power of our presidency and the struggle to end the Iraq war in a way that doesn't continue to destabilize the Middle East. All of this is taking place in a global cauldron where America's moral authority — our guiding compass — has continued to decline in the eyes of enemies and allies alike. It's no small coincidence that these events corresponded with the rise of 24-hour media and sensationalist journalism.

Overall, Americans have become less trusting of institutions and individuals — government, media and each other. And most recently, the nation witnessed a negative presidential campaign that was littered with personal attacks on individual character, a bitter divide over responses to terrorism, war and the state of our economy. President Bush won a second term in the White House by a 51 to 48 percent margin in the popular vote and 286 to 252 in the Electoral College. Bush's razor-thin margin of victory in the popular vote follows Election 2000, which was one of the closest in history. Clearly, America is narrowly divided along political, personal and moral lines that decided the outcome of this election.

The 2008 election was wide open at the start as more and more Americans fall into the independent column. And the race began earlier and money is pouring into campaign coffers at a fundraising rate that is already on pace to smash the totals for previous elections. This is all taking place while Americans grapple with issues like global warming and a perpetual war on terrorism. All these issues have world-altering implications. Who leads us next is of great importance and, it is hoped, will be a catalyst for renewed voter engagement.

But as outlined throughout this book, countless barriers exist that turn citizens off from politics or keep them away from the civic process entirely. A cycle of neglect exists, where citizens don't vote, contact their elected officials about important issues or contribute to, or get involved in political campaigns. Elected officials are often too busy to chase down the disinterested and disengaged. As a result, they focus on the issues of the citizens already active in the system and not those who've shown limited interest in the process. The cycle becomes a self-fulfilling prophecy of distrust, miscommunication and disengagement.

Politics have become increasingly partisan and bitter. And many Americans feel that real discussions of issues are subverted because of negative attacks or are controlled by special interest groups. Further, they see long lines at the polls (because of an inefficient system, and not staggering turnout), at the motor vehicle department and other government institutions, and decide that they don't have the time to participate. These institutional barriers make government seem unwelcoming and cumbersome, turning people away from the process.

As America has grown and changed, we've lost a sense of civic responsibility. Members of the Greatest Generation regularly discussed politics and civic issues with their families, lessons that were reinforced in school. But Vietnam tore families and communities apart. And it embittered a generation of adults, the Baby Boomers, many of whom failed to pass on a civic legacy to their children. Many even encouraged their children to find a different path, one that didn't include participating in a system that couldn't meet their needs and dreams. In this void, America's youth have grown up distrusting of government and prefer to pursue more individual activities, instead of taking part in the civic process. As a result, more than half of Generations X and Y fail to regularly vote, and even fewer percentages are informed about issues of importance to society even though they regularly volunteer.

If these barriers weren't enough, countless personal obstacles exist that create challenges to active civic participation. Many Americans simply feel that they don't have enough nonpartisan, unbiased information to make decisions or to know where to begin engaging with government. The Internet provides a wealth of information on candidates, issues, government and the civic process. Yet it is increasingly difficult to quickly and easily find valuable information because there is just so much to wade through.

The chaotic lifestyle of today's American family also presents personal barriers to participation. From longer commutes and more time in the office, to soccer games, play practice and a host of other activities — America's families are pulled in a million directions each day. As a result, the civic process takes a back seat to more familial and career-oriented matters.

Television and the Internet also play critical roles in our collective civic decline. The average American now watches nearly four hours of TV *every day*. Combine that total with at least eight hours of work or school, family activities, etc., and volunteerism, participating in community groups and voting all become secondary agenda items. Television has also isolated people and made them more passive as we sit alone in the dark, devouring reality and crime investigation programming, and the details about Hollywood's "prostitots," who are either caught partying or being shuffled from jail to rehab.

It is still too early to decipher the impact Internet activity will have on civic engagement. Some experts hold the Internet up as the great political equalizer and a vehicle for connecting people around the world. It certainly allows individuals to remain in contact, and political campaigns are beginning to leverage its power for fundraising and educational purposes. But so far, the relationships built online seem relatively weak and can't replace face-to-face contact and knee cap-to-knee cap discussions of politics and community issues. These activities help to make the process personal for people. Online interaction also produces lower thresholds of trust, which is a cornerstone of community-building and civic activity.

People point to a bright future for the Internet as a political tool because candidates raised significant amounts of campaign money in 2004 and 2006, and are off to a fast start for 2008. Yes, it has been a tool for organizing small segments of active and educated individuals. But unfortunately, the Internet proved to be an ineffective vehicle for mobilizing people to action — even those who contributed to political campaigns. The 2008 presidential elections are following a similar upward trajectory of online donating. Turnout in this critical election will provide greater insight into the value and power of virtual education and organizing.

Countless organizations have attempted to tackle the problem of diminishing engagement in recent years. As a result of their work, millions of people have registered to vote, become more informed about candidates and issues, volunteered in their communities and heeded the call to action — all very positive outcomes. Yet at the same time, indicators of America's civic health have fluctuated. Volunteerism is finally ticking up again after dipping in the wake of 9/11. Voter turnout increased in 2004 and slightly in 2006, but entire segments of citizens continue to remain disengaged.

The above litany of negative indicators paints a frightening picture of American civic health if we continue to bicker and fail to address the status quo. Yet I remain optimistic that people want to be engaged, and that they care about issues impacting communities at home and around the world. They want to take part in elections and in government. It's just that too many of us don't feel welcomed into the system or possess the basic tools for effective participation. Working in government, educating the community about critical issues and empowering people to be informed and active voters provided countless examples of America at its finest. I saw firsthand that people will engage when government, elections and community problems have direct meaning to their daily lives — and they need to be accessible.

Historians and scholars will look upon the 2004, 2006 and 2008 elections as a turning point. These media-driven campaigns pit candidates and parties with deep ideological divides against each other, forcing Americans to take sides on very serious matters: for gay rights or against them; supportive of the Iraq War or sure that the conflict lessened our security and destabilized the Middle East; love the president or loathe him; support greater religious influence in government or back the separation of church and state; and countless other distinctions. Unfortunately today, American political discourse consists of elected officials, candidates and their spokespeople or talking heads shouting at each other instead of listening and actually debating issues. They try to score points with bumper sticker slogans or by putting down their opponent. The conversations on CNN, FOX News and countless other mediums are more about style and less about substance. The participants definitely are not interested in actually solving the topic or problem being discussed. The goal is to simply stick to the party line and convince the viewer or listener that your idea is the right one and that the guy on the other side is flat out wrong! The person offering the counter argument might as well not even be there because the two participants aren't trying to convince the other, or to solve anything.

If you take the time to listen to politicians today, you'd be left with the impression that Democrats are from Venus and Republicans are from Mars. Members of each party point out how wrong the other is on any given topic and how that view is completely contrary to what Americans want or need. You will often hear lines like "my Democratic (or Republican) colleague is deeply out of touch with mainstream America."

But at the end of the day, the legislation that is produced and actually passes in Congress is fairly, middle of the road stuff. The majority of legislation that gets signed into law is really what Americans are asking for or need. But to hear the issue discussed on the front end, you'd think the two parties would never be able to reach agreement on what to have for lunch, let alone the federal budget. Yet when they get around to it, elected officials across America actually pass bills that consist of consensus and compromise. And that is how our Founding Fathers wanted things: Congress produces an American legislative ship that tacks from side-to-side. But it never veers wildly in a new direction (obviously there are some recent exceptions to this rule, like the Iraq "conflict").

Recent close elections at all levels of government prove that Americans have strong opinions about the state of the world and the issues of our day. But they are evenly divided on which party is best equipped to move us in the right direction. A big explanation for this is the situation outlined above. The rhetoric of these candidates comes from the extreme poles of politics. But when it comes down to it, there isn't a dimes worth of difference between the results the parties actually produce.

America is at a crossroads. We're evenly divided but deeply disengaged. The situation presents a unique opportunity to drastically change the state of civic participation in this country. People do care and they do want to be involved in the political process. They are thirsty for leaders who will rise above rhetoric and partisanship to talk honestly and openly about the issues and challenges that face us as communities, cities, states and a nation. They will rally behind people who invite them into the process by making the debates and institutions of government accessible, meaningful and personal.

But America and the world can't wait. One of the most amazing things about our government is the right and responsibility to take part in its operations. We are given unalienable rights to speak our minds, to influence and elect our leaders and to guide the direction in which our national ship sails. But with this liberty comes the responsibility of taking action and making our voices heard.

We as Americans can't wait for leaders to come to us. We can't wait for them to bring government to our doorstep. It's not in their interest to do that. And participation isn't some entitlement anyway. It is a right, but we are required to work for it. And volunteering isn't an alternative that will bring the problems facing our country to an end. Yes, we must volunteer in our communities, but that service must be met with active political engagement. The challenges we face will be solved when we serve our communities *and* vote *and* remain active in the debates in the halls of government following each election. It is a loop of participation that must be closed to ensure the challenges, needs and opportunities within our communities are met.

Each of us must take part. We all must be leaders in our own right. By working together we can reap the benefits and the boundless opportunity available in our country. And taking part in the civic process is as easy as one, two, three *and* four! The first step to active citizenship is becoming educated. Learn about the issues, how government works and share that information with others. Read newspapers, surf the net and attend forums and community meetings to become educated about issues and the needs of your community.

The second step is finding others. True political power comes from identifying people who think and feel the way you do about a given issue and working together to bring about change. But being informed and having a coalition of like-minded individuals isn't quite enough to influence the political process. It's also necessary to build relationships with our elected officials. They want and need our input, especially at the local and state levels where there is less of a staff structure for educating elected officials about the countless issues they vote on each day.

These three steps — getting informed, finding others and getting to know your elected officials — aren't easy and they take time. But they are the necessary ingredients for bringing about change, solving problems and ultimately, helping us to realize America's bright future. Yet these steps alone aren't enough either. As Americans, it is a paramount responsibility that we exercise the rights provided us by the Constitution and Declaration of Independence. And to do that *you must take action*, which is the final requirement of citizenship. Taking action simply means putting the knowledge and relationships developed through active civic engagement to work for our families, neighborhoods, country and world.

And so, no matter what issues drive you — a healthy environment, better schools, safer streets, gun owners' rights or security from terror — taking action is the only way to make your voice heard. The form of action or results isn't what matters: Send a letter to your local newspaper, call your Congressman, volunteer, inform a neighbor, bring your children to the polls when voting or participate in a protest or rally. The point is that by acting, you're engaged in the civic process and have a voice in the outcomes of government. Hopefully this book has provided the tools and inspiration for taking the lead in bringing about change. Take part in your own liberty and join me in the trenches!

Citations

Charleston — Charleston Gazette Editorial Board, *Civic lessons lost to youth* (Charleston: Charleston Newspapers, 2003)

Chetwynd — Josh Chetwynd and Kevin Whitelaw, *Young voters: up for grabs* (New York, US News & World Report, 1996)

CNN — CNN News, *Tom Brokaw and the Greatest Generation* (Atlanta, CNN News, 2000)

CNN — CNN News, *How we get here: a timeline of the Florida recount* (Atlanta, CNN, 2000)

CNN — CNN News, *Poll: Majority of Americans accept Bush as legitimate president* (Washington: CNN Politics, 2001)

CNN — CNN News, *Rock the vote: Young, older voters split on issues* (Atlanta: CNN, 2003)

Davis — Richard J. Davis, *Watergate, a look back* (New York, New York Law Journal, 2002)

Drinkard — Jim Drinkard and Jill Lawrence, *Online, off and running: Web a new campaign front* (Alexandria, VA: USA Today, 2003)

Federal — Federal Elections Commission, *Voter Registration and Turnout in Federal Elections* (Washington: Federal Elections Commission, 2005)

Feldmeth — Greg D. Feldmeth, *A chronology of the Watergate Crisis* (Pasadena, CA: Polytechnic School US History Resources, 1998)

Foote — Donna Foote, *Islam, Arabic and Afghanistan 101* (New York: Newsweek, 2001)

Frisardi — Raquel Frisardi, *Poll finds most Princeton students support Iraq War* (Princeton: Princetonian, 2002)

Greenberg — Stanley B. Greenberg, *The Youth Vote Project* (Washington, D.C.: Democratic Leadership Council Report, 1996)

Gubbins — Teresa Gubbins, *Generation Y knows what's hot, who's cool and how to spend a ton of money* (Dallas: Dallas Morning News, 1999)

Guterbock — Thomas M. Guterbock and John C. Fries, *Maintaining America's Social Fabric: The AARP Survey of Civic Involvement* (Washington, D.C.: American Association of Retired Persons, 1997)

Hawkes — Lt. Col. Greg Hawkes, *We could learn something from "greatest generation"* (Seymour Johnson Air Force base, NC: 336th Fighter Squadron paper, 2001)

History — Historytimeline.com, *1970-1979* (Washington, D.C.: history-timeline.com, 2006)

Hollander — Barry Hollander, *The New News and the 1992 Presidential Campaign: Perceived vs. Actual Political Knowledge* (Washington, D.C.: Journalism & Mass Communications Quarterly, 1995)

Horne — Christopher Horne, *Social Capital in Metropolitan Atlanta* (Atlanta, The Community Foundation for greater Atlanta, 2001)

Kaiser — Robert Kaiser, *We can't bury 'nam under the memorial* (Washington: The Washington Post, 1982)

Kraske — Steve Kraske, *Civic Lessons Pay Dividends* (Kansas City, The Kansas City Star, 2003)

Kraut — Robert Kraut, Vicki Lundmark, Patterson, Kiesler, Mukopadhyay and Scherlis, *Internet Paradox: A social technology that reduces social involvement and psychological well-being* (Pittsburgh, Carnegie Mellon University, 2000)

Losyk — Bob Losyk, *Generation X: what they think and what they plan to do* (New York: Public Management, 1997)

Mai — Anne Mai, *Youth vote a 'sleeping giant'* (Los Angeles: UCLA Daily Bruin, 1996)

Marlantes — Liz Marlantes, *In race for the presidency, Democrat Howard Dean is turning heads with online money-making prowess* (Washington, D.C.: Christian Science Monitor, 2003)

McCaleb — Christopher McCaleb, *Bush, now president-elect, signals will to bridge partisan gap* (Washington: CNN Politics, 2000)

McLaughlin — Abraham McLaughlin, *Return of college peaceniks* (Dallas: Christian Science Monitor, 2002)

Meacham — Jon Meacham, *The truth about twenty-somethings* (Washington, D.C.: The Washington Monthly, 1995)

Mills — Michael P. Mills, *Youth voter registration movement: Flashy campaign, limited results* (Atlanta, Georgia State University, 1999)

Moseley — Matthew Moseley, *The youth service movement: America's trump card in revitalizing democracy* (Washington, D.C.: National Civic Review, 1995)

Naughton — Keith Naughton, *Generation 9-11* (New York: Newsweek, 2001)

Newell — Marilou Newell, *"Greatest Generation knows the meaning of sacrifice"* (South Carolina: South Coast Today, 2001)

Non-Profit — Non-Profit Voter Engagement Network, *America goes to the polls: A report on voter turnout in the 2006 Election* (St. Paul, MN: Non-Profit Voter Engagement, 2007)

O'Toole — Kathleen O'Toole, *Study offers early look at how Internet is changing daily life* (Stanford: Stanford Institute for the Quantitative Study of Society, 2000)

Pieper — Chris Pieper, *Decision 2000: How cynical will the press be this time* (New York: BraveNews World 2000, 2000)

Pierre — Robert E. Pierre, *Students across US mount antiwar protests* (Washington: The Washington post, 2003)

Putnam — Robert D. Putnam, *The strange disappearance of Civic America* (Washington, D.C.: The American Prospect, 1996)

Reader's — Reader's Digest, *Exposing the myth of the generation gap* (New York, Reader's Digest, 1995)

Reader's — Reader's Digest, *Landmark Reader's Digest survey reveals new American Paradox* (Pleasantville, NY: Reader's Digest, 2003)

Rubenstein and Smith — Lori Rubenstein and Burck Smith, *Voter Participation: A state report* (Washington, D.C.: Center for Policy Alternatives, 1993)

Samuels — Allison Samuels, *They know I'm about something* (New York: Newsweek, 2001)

Santich — Kate Santich, *Cynicism Reigns: We find ourselves dwelling in the land of the free and the home of the disillusioned. But really, who cares?* (Orlando: Orlando Sentinel, 2003)

Schabner — Dean Schabner, *Hard work: Downturn or not, Americans spend more time on the job than anyone* (New York, ABC News, 2003)

Schneider — Bill Schneider, *Cynicism didn't start with Watergate* (Washington: CNN Politics, 1997)

Smith — J. Walker Smith and Ann Clurman, *Excerpt from Rocking the Ages* (New York, Time Magazine, 1997)

Soule — Suzanne Soule, *Will they engage? Political knowledge, participation and attitudes of Generations X and Y* (Washington: German and American Conference, 2001)

St. Louis — St. Louis Post Dispatch Editorial Board, *The Greatest Generation* (St. Louis, MO: St. Louis Post Dispatch, 1999)

Stahelski — Anthony Stahelski, *A long-overdue tribute to the Greatest Generation* (Seattle: The Times, 2000)

Tabernacle Group — Lake Snell Perry and Associate, *Short Term Impacts, Long Term Opportunities: The political and civic engagement of young adults in America* (Washington, D.C.: Center for Democracy & Citizenship and the Partnership for Trust in Government at the Council of Excellence in Government, 2002)

Texas — The Texas Transportation Institute, *The Urban Mobility Report: New congestion study shows remedies working, but traffic jams still growing* (College Station, TX: The Texas Ttansportation Institute, 2002)

Torres — Daniel de Torres, *Chronology of the war in Vietnam* (Virginia, 2004)

Trigaux — Robert Trigaux, *Bending business attitudes to appeal to Generation Y* (St. Petersburg: St. Petersburg Times, 2003)

Tull — Susie Tull, *Howard Dean uses Convio to raise $7.4 million online in third quarter* (Austin, TX: Charitywire, 2003)

Wikipedia — Wikipedia online, *Greatest Generation* (New York, Wikipedia. com, 2005)

Wikipedia — Wikipedia online, *History of World War II* (New York, Wikipedia.com, 2005)

Wikipedia — Wikipedia online, *The 1950s, 1960s, 1970s* (New York, Wikipedia.com, 2005)

Yaffee — Robert A. Yaffee, *Presidential Scandals and Job Approval* (New York, New York University, 2004)

www.ingramcontent.com/pod-product-compliance
Lightning Source LLC
Chambersburg PA
CBHW070839310526
45793CB00010B/24